stencilling

stencilling
A creative home guide

Sacha Cohen
Photography by Adrian Taylor

southwater

This edition is published by Southwater

Distributed in the UK by
The Manning Partnership
251–253 London Road East
Batheaston
Bath BA1 7RL
UK
tel. (0044) 01225 852 727
fax. (0044) 01225 852 852

Distributed in the USA by
Ottenheimer Publishing
5 Park Center Court
Suite 300
Owing Mills MD 2117-5001
USA
tel. (001) 410 902 9100
fax. (001) 410 902 7210

Distributed in Australia by
Sandstone Publishing
Unit 1, 360 Norton Street
Leichhardt
New South Wales 2040
Australia
tel. (0061) 2 9560 7888
fax. (0061) 2 9560 7488

Distributed in New Zealand by
Five Mile Press NZ
PO Box 33-1071
Takapuna
Auckland 9
New Zealand
tel. (0064) 9 4444 144
fax. (0064) 9 4444 518

All rights reserved. No part of this publication may be reproduced, stored in a retrieval system, or transmitted in any way or by any means, electronic, mechanical, photocopying, recording or otherwise, without prior written permission of the copyright holder.

Southwater is an imprint of
Anness Publishing Limited
© 1997, 2000 Anness Publishing Limited

1 3 5 7 9 10 8 6 4 2

Publisher: Joanna Lorenz
Senior Editor: Lindsay Porter
Designer: Bobbie Colgate Stone
Photographer: Adrian Taylor
Illustrators: Madeleine David and Lucinda Ganderton

Previously published as *Inspirations: Stencilling*

CONTENTS

Introduction	6
Frosted Vases	8
Painted Drawers	11
Art Nouveau Hatbox	14
Star Frame	17
Making Sandcastles	20
Seashore Bathroom Set	24
Greek Urns	27
Pennsylvania Dutch Tulips	30
French Country Kitchen	34
Tray of Autumn Leaves	38
Gilded Candles	41
Renaissance Art	44
Geometric Floor Tiles	48
Organza Cushion	52
Tablecloth and Napkins	55
Through the Grapevine	58
Rope and Shells	62
Heraldic Dining Room	66
Trompe L'œil Plates	70
Celestial Cherubs	74
Materials	78
Equipment	80
Basic Techniques	82
Templates	87
Suppliers & Acknowledgments	95
Index	96

INTRODUCTION

Stenciling was the first paint effect that I ever tried, and I remember being amazed at how quick and easy it was. Stenciling has been used in interior design for centuries, either to add delicate decoration to a grand scheme or as an alternative to expensive wallpapers. Today we are witnessing a revival in the art of stenciling, with stencils and paints for every surface now widely available.

This book is designed to inspire you to experiment with stenciling while at the same time adding an individual touch to your home. Stenciling is more than the mere act of adding a splash of color to an otherwise plain room: It is an art in its own right and, furthermore, one that enables you to create a decorative effect that would be impossible to achieve by any other means. It is a simple, cheap and impressive way of decorating any surface. Stencils are highly adaptable and can be used on items large and small to give them character. You will be pleasantly surprised by how little time it takes to transform even the largest surface with a pattern.

This book features clear step-by-step photography to guide you through basic stenciling techniques, then moves on to larger projects for more experienced craft artists. All the patterns for the stencils are included, together with information on materials required. Every medium is covered, including stenciling on fabrics, floors, walls and glass, as well as special tips for every surface. Designs range from heraldic patterns to seashore motifs. Experiment with colors: You can transform a pattern by using either subtle or bright shades. Finally, a word of warning: Once you find out just how easy stenciling can be, it may be very difficult to stop.

Deborah Barker

STENCILING

FROSTED VASES

Give colored or clear glass vases a designer touch by using glass-etching cream and reverse stenciling. The shapes are cut from adhesive-backed plastic and removed after stenciling to reveal the clear outlines. Opt for flowers and leaves, stripes or polka dots—the choice is yours. The same technique could be used to transform windows.

YOU WILL NEED
glass vase
adhesive-backed plastic
scissors
rubber gloves
glass-etching cream
soft paintbrush

1 Wash the vase with hot soapy water to remove any grease. Let the vase dry. Trace the flower and leaf templates at the back of the book and transfer them to the back of a piece of adhesive-backed plastic. Cut out the shapes with scissors.

2 Decide where you want to position the shapes on the vase, remove the backing paper and stick in place, smoothing them down.

3 Wearing rubber gloves, paint the etching cream evenly over the outside of the vase with a paintbrush, and let dry in a warm, dust-free area for about 30 minutes.

4 Still wearing the rubber gloves, wash the cream off the vase with warm water and let dry. If there are blotchy areas where the cream hasn't worked, simply paint the vase again and let it sit for another 30 minutes. When you are happy with the results, peel off the plastic shapes and wash the vase again to remove any sticky smears left by the plastic.

5 For a smaller vase, try using just one motif. Paint on the etching cream in the same way as for the large vase and let it sit for 30 minutes.

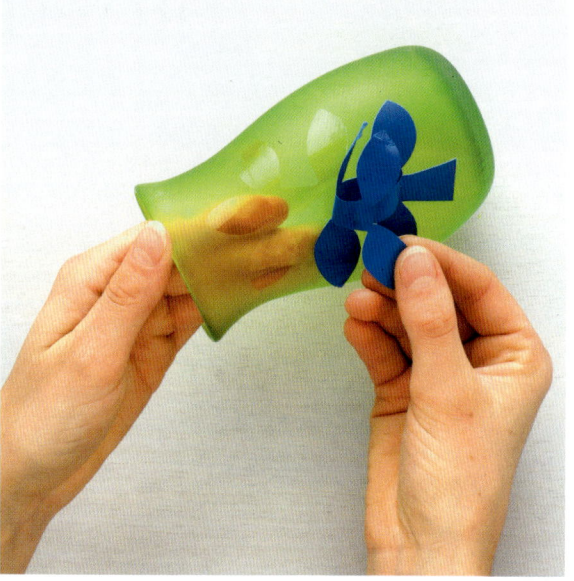

6 Wash off the etching cream and peel off the plastic motif to reveal the design, then wash the vase again.

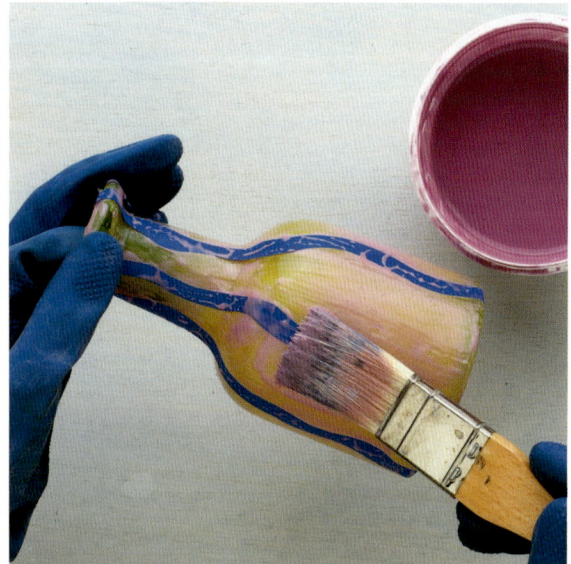

7 For a striped frosted vase, cut out straight or curved strips of adhesive-backed plastic and stick them on the vase. Paint on the etching cream as before and let dry for 30 minutes.

8 Wash off the etching cream, then peel off the plastic strips and wash the vase again to remove any sticky smears left by the plastic.

STENCILING

PAINTED DRAWERS

Jazz up plain, unfinished drawers with bright paint-box colors and simple daisy stencils. The same stencils could be used to decorate larger pieces of furniture, such as a chest of drawers for a child's room, or to update plain kitchen units. Small pots of latex paint are ideal to use on small projects.

YOU WILL NEED
set of wooden drawers
sandpaper
latex paints in various colors
paintbrush
screwdriver
acetate
craft knife and cutting mat
stencil brush
matte acrylic varnish
white glue (optional)

1 Remove the drawers and sand down the frame and drawers to remove any rough areas or patches of old paint.

2 Paint the drawer frame using latex paint and a paintbrush. Let dry, then apply a second coat of paint.

3 Unscrew the drawer knobs and paint each drawer in a different-colored latex paint. Let dry and apply a second coat. Trace the flower template at the back of the book and cut a stencil from acetate as described in the basic techniques.

4 When the drawers are dry, position the flower stencil in the center of a drawer and, using a stencil brush and paint in a contrasting color, stencil on the flower. Let dry.

5 Stencil a flower in the center of each drawer, using a different color for each one.

PAINTED DRAWERS

6 Paint the drawer knobs with two coats of paint, letting them dry between coats. Let dry.

7 Screw or glue a painted knob to the center of each drawer. Varnish the drawers with matte acrylic varnish. Let dry before reassembling.

STENCILING

ART NOUVEAU HATBOX

An elegantly stenciled hatbox and matching shoe bag would be perfect for storing a bride's hat and shoes. Make a set for yourself or to give to someone special. And you don't have to stop there: Stencil a whole stack of matching hatboxes to use for stylish storage in a bedroom.

YOU WILL NEED
round hatbox
white primer
paintbrushes
water-based wood wash in pale green
tape measure
pencil
stencil cardboard
craft knife and cutting mat
ruler
spray adhesive
stencil brushes
stencil paints in dark green, royal blue and pale green

1 Paint the hatbox with two coats of white primer. Dilute one part pale green wood wash with one part water and apply two or three light washes to the hatbox, letting them dry between coats. Measure the circumference of the box and divide by six or eight. Lightly mark the measurements on the lid and side of the box with a pencil.

2 Trace the flower and heart templates at the back of the book. Cut the stencils from stencil cardboard as described in the basic techniques. Mark a pencil line across the bottom of the stencil to help align it on the box. Spray lightly with adhesive and position on the box. Using a stencil brush and dark green stencil paint, stencil the leaves and stem. Remove the stencil when dry, respray with adhesive and reposition. Continue to work around the box.

3 Reposition the stencil on the leaves, and add shadow to the points where the leaves meet the stem using royal blue paint. Use a clean brush to keep the colors clean.

ART NOUVEAU HATBOX

4 Using the single heart stencil, add a pale green heart between each pair of leaves.

5 Stencil blossoms around the rim of the lid in dark green, adding a royal blue shadow as before. Stencil the flower motif in the center of the lid.

6 Add pale green heart motifs around the main motif, using a very small amount of paint for a delicate touch.

Above: Stencil a matching calico shoe bag, using fabric paints, to protect a treasured pair of shoes.

16

STENCILING

STAR FRAME

Give plain or old picture frames a new look with textured stars. Adding ready-mixed filler to acrylic stencil paint gives a three-dimensional effect to stenciled designs. Once you have mixed your plaster you will need to work quickly before it sets.

YOU WILL NEED
wooden picture frame
latex paints in dark and light blue
paintbrush
soft cloth
wax furniture polish
sandpaper
acetate
craft knife and cutting mat
bowl
ready-mixed filler
acrylic paint in dark blue
stencil brush
flowerpots

1 Paint the frame in dark blue latex paint using a paintbrush. When dry, apply a second coat and let dry.

2 Using a soft cloth, rub wax furniture polish all over the frame and let dry.

3 Paint the frame with light blue latex paint and let dry. Paint on a second coat and let dry. Then lightly sand the frame to create a distressed effect.

STAR FRAME

4 Cut a large and a small star stencil from acetate as described in the basic techniques. In a bowl, combine the ready-mixed filler and acrylic paint until you are happy with the shade, remembering that when the filler dries it will be much lighter.

5 Position the star stencil on the frame and dab on the filler with a stencil brush. Keep stenciling until you have covered the frame. Let the filler harden and wash the brush thoroughly.

6 When the filler has dried and hardened, gently smooth the stars with sandpaper.

7 Paint and stencil the flowerpots in the same way as the picture frame.

STENCILING

MAKING SANDCASTLES

Evocative of childhood summers spent on the beach, sandcastles are simple, colorful shapes to stencil. Perfect for a child's room or for a family bathroom, they will bring a touch of humor to your walls. Paint the flags in different colors or glue on paper flags for added interest.

YOU WILL NEED
latex paints in blue and white
paintbrush
household sponge
acetate
craft knife and cutting mat
tape measure
pencil
masking tape
stencil paints in yellow, black and other colors of your choice
stencil brushes
fine paintbrush
colored paper (optional)
white glue (optional)

1 Paint below chair-rail height in blue. When dry, rub on white latex with a sponge. Trace the templates at the back of the book. Cut out the stencils from acetate as described in the basic techniques.

2 Measure the wall to calculate how many sandcastles you can fit on it and make light pencil marks at regular intervals. Position the stencil above the chair rail and secure the corners with masking tape.

3 Using yellow stencil paint and a stencil brush, stencil in the first sandcastle.

MAKING SANDCASTLES

4 Stencil each flag in a different color and remove the stencil.

5 When the paint has dried, stencil a star on the sandcastle in a contrasting color of paint.

6 Using a fine paintbrush and black stencil paint, paint in the flagpoles.

7 Continue stenciling the sandcastles along the wall, using your pencil marks to position them. ▶

MAKING SANDCASTLES

8 As an alternative to stenciling the flags, cut out triangles of colored paper and glue them to the wall with white glue, then paint in the flagpoles.

Above: Don't be too exacting when painting the flagpoles. Crooked lines and erratic angles add to the childlike quality of the sandcastle frieze.

Left: A variation on the seashore theme might include bright tropical shapes in Caribbean colors.

STENCILING

SEASHORE BATHROOM SET

Seaside themes are always popular for a bathroom, and these stencils in fresh blue and white link the different elements of the room. For best results, choose paints to suit the surface you are planning to stencil: enamel paint for plastic and glass and fabric paint for the towels.

YOU WILL NEED
acetate
craft knife and cutting mat
clear plastic shower curtain
stencil brush
enamel paints in white and blue
smooth cotton hand towel
fabric paint in dark blue
iron
2 glass tumblers
masking tape (optional)

1 Trace the shell, starfish and fish templates at the back of the book. Cut the stencils from acetate as described in the basic techniques. Lay the shower curtain on a flat surface. Lightly dab the stencil brush in the white enamel paint and begin to stencil the shapes on the curtain.

2 Continue to stencil the shapes randomly over the whole shower curtain, taking care not to overload the brush with paint. Let dry.

3 Reposition the stencils on the painted shapes and dab on the blue paint. Leave some of the shapes white. Let the curtain dry before hanging it in place.

4 Lay the hand towel on a flat surface. Using the fish stencil and dark blue fabric paint, stencil a border of fish across one short edge of the towel.

5 Stencil the opposite edge of the towel, arranging the fish in a different way. Iron the towel to set the fabric paint, following the manufacturer's instructions.

SEASHORE BATHROOM SET

6 For the glass, hold or tape the fish stencil in place and gently dab on white enamel paint.

7 Let dry, then reposition the stencil and continue to stencil fish all over the glass. Decorate the second glass with blue fish. The glasses should be used only for decoration; do not apply enamel paints to surfaces that will be eaten from.

Above: Blue and white stencils work well in a plain white bathroom. You can also choose colors to coordinate with your existing decor.

STENCILING

GREEK URNS

Classic Greek urns softly outlined under a warm terra-cotta wash have a very Mediterranean feel. The stenciling is done in clear varnish so that the top color slides over without adhering, leaving subtly colored motifs. Arrange the urns randomly over the wall for an informal finish.

YOU WILL NEED
latex paints in cream and terra-cotta
large household sponge
acetate
craft knife and cutting mat
masking tape
stencil brush
satin acrylic varnish
wallpaper paste
cloth

1 Working in rough, sweeping strokes, rub a base coat of warm cream latex over the wall using a sponge. Trace the urn template at the back of the book and cut out a stencil from acetate as described in the basic techniques. Tape it to the wall and stencil with clear acrylic varnish. Reposition the stencil and cover the wall with randomly arranged urns.

2 Make the wallpaper paste following the instructions on the package. Mix one part terra-cotta latex with one part paste. This will make the wash viscous and slow down the drying time so as to prevent "seams" in the finished wash. Using a sponge, dab lumps of the mixture over a 3-foot square area of the wall.

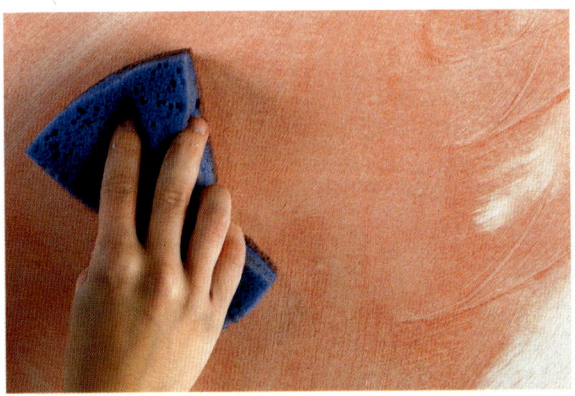

3 Immediately rub the wall in a circular motion to blur the sponge marks.

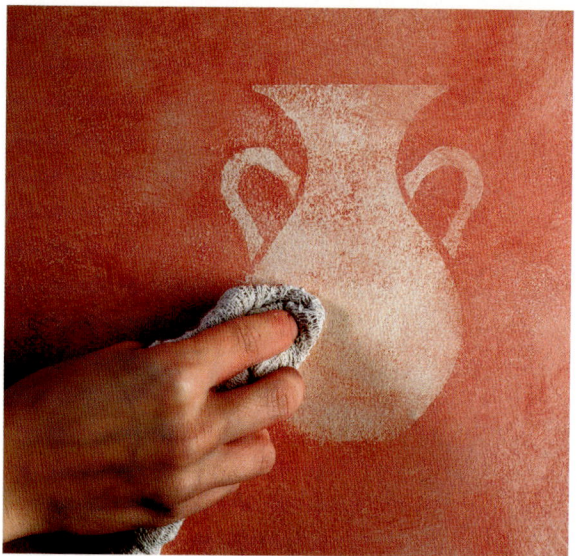

4 Continue dabbing on paint and blurring with the sponge to cover the whole wall. The varnished urns should be revealed underneath the wash.

5 If the urns are not clear enough, use a slightly damp cloth and your index finger to rub off a little more wash from the varnished shape. This can be done even when the wall has dried or after the room has been completed.

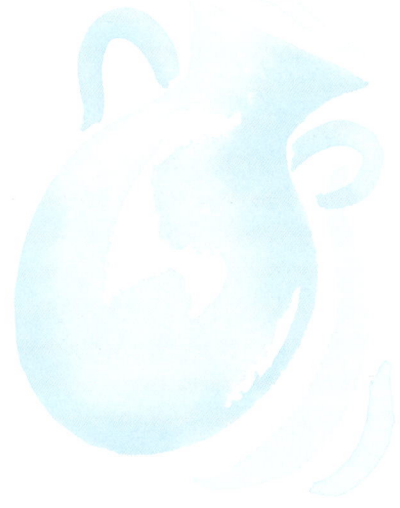

Left: Try washing duck-egg blue over a beige background as an alternative color combination.

STENCILING

PENNSYLVANIA DUTCH TULIPS

This American folk art-inspired idea uses the rich colors and simple motifs beloved by the German and Dutch immigrants to Pennsylvania. Create the effect of hand-painted wallpaper or, for a beginner's project, take a single motif and use it to decorate a small cupboard.

YOU WILL NEED
latex paint in dark ocher
large and small paintbrushes
wood wash in indigo blue and mulberry
stencil cardboard
craft knife and cutting mat
pencil
ruler
stencil brushes
stencil paints in red, light green, dark green and pale brown
saucer or cloth
artist's paintbrush

1 Dilute one part ocher latex with one part water. Using a large paintbrush, cover the top half of the wall with the diluted latex. Use vertical brushstrokes for an even texture.

2 Paint the lower half of the wall with indigo blue wash. Finish with a curving line using a dry brush to suggest wood grain.

3 Paint the chair rail or a strip at chair-rail height in mulberry wash using a narrow brush to give a clean edge.

4 Trace the tulip and heart templates at the back of the book and cut the stencils from stencil cardboard as described in the basic techniques. Mark the center of each edge of the stencil. Measure the wall and divide it into equal sections, so that the repeats will fall at about 8-inch intervals. Mark the positions lightly with pencil, so that they can be erased later.

5 Dip the stencil brush into red stencil paint. Rub the brush on a saucer or cloth until it is almost dry before stenciling in the tulips. Let dry.

6 Paint the leaves in light green stencil paint with darker green shading. Paint the stems in dark green using an artist's paintbrush. Let dry.

7 Stencil the basket in pale brown stencil paint using a chunky stencil brush.

PENNSYLVANIA DUTCH TULIPS

8 Stencil a single heart between each set of two baskets of tulips using red stencil paint.

Below: Make a matching cupboard following the same method and using just one motif.

Above: A stenciled motif on a functional kitchen storage tin gives instant folk-art style.

STENCILING

FRENCH COUNTRY KITCHEN

This curtain design is adapted from the pattern on a French Art Deco soup bowl found at a flea market in Brussels. The flower design is also echoed in the hand-stenciled tiles and goes perfectly with the simple checkerboard border for a country look.

YOU WILL NEED
FOR THE CURTAIN:
white muslin (see measuring)
iron
newspaper
masking tape
stencil cardboard
craft knife and cutting mat
spray adhesive
solid stencil paint in blue
stencil brush
pressing cloth
needle
white cotton thread
tape measure
dressmaker's chalk
white cotton tape
small pearl buttons
FOR THE TILES:
4-inch-square white tiles
spray paint in red

MEASURING
To calculate the amount of muslin, allow 1.5 times the width of the window plus 1 inch for each side hem, and add 3 inches to the length for hems.

1 Press the muslin to remove any creases, then fold it lengthwise in accordion folds. Press lightly to mark the creases, then fold it horizontally in accordion folds and press again. These squares will act as a guide for positioning the motifs. Cover the work surface with newspaper and tape down the muslin so that it is taut.

2 Trace the three floral templates and the border template at the back of the book and cut out the stencils from stencil cardboard as described in the basic techniques. Spray the back of one stencil with adhesive and, starting at the top right, lightly stencil the first motif.

34

3 Alternating the stencils as you work, stencil flowers in every other square over the whole curtain, leaving 6 inches free at the lower edge.

4 Stencil the blue checkerboard border along the bottom, lining up the stencil each time by matching the last two squares of the previous motif with the first two of the next stencil. Press the fabric well using a pressing cloth and iron.

5 Press under and slip-stitch a ½-inch double hem around the sides and lower edge. Make a 1-inch double hem along the top edge.

6 Measure the top edge of the curtain and, using dressmaker's chalk, mark it into sections about 8 inches apart. Cut a 10-inch piece of cotton tape for each mark. Fold the first piece of tape in half and stitch it to the back of the first mark. Sew a button onto the front of the curtain to anchor the tape. Repeat all the way along the edge and then tie the finished curtain onto the curtain pole in bows.

FRENCH COUNTRY KITCHEN

Above: The simple tape ties that attach the curtain to the pole provide an attractively rustic finish.

7 For the tiles, cut a piece of stencil cardboard to fit the tile. Cut out the three floral stencils as before, using a craft knife and a cutting mat.

8 Cover the work surface with newspaper. Using red spray paint, spray over the stencil lightly and evenly. Let dry, then remove the stencil.

Above: The coordinating tiles can be used individually as trivets or set in the wall among plain white tiles.

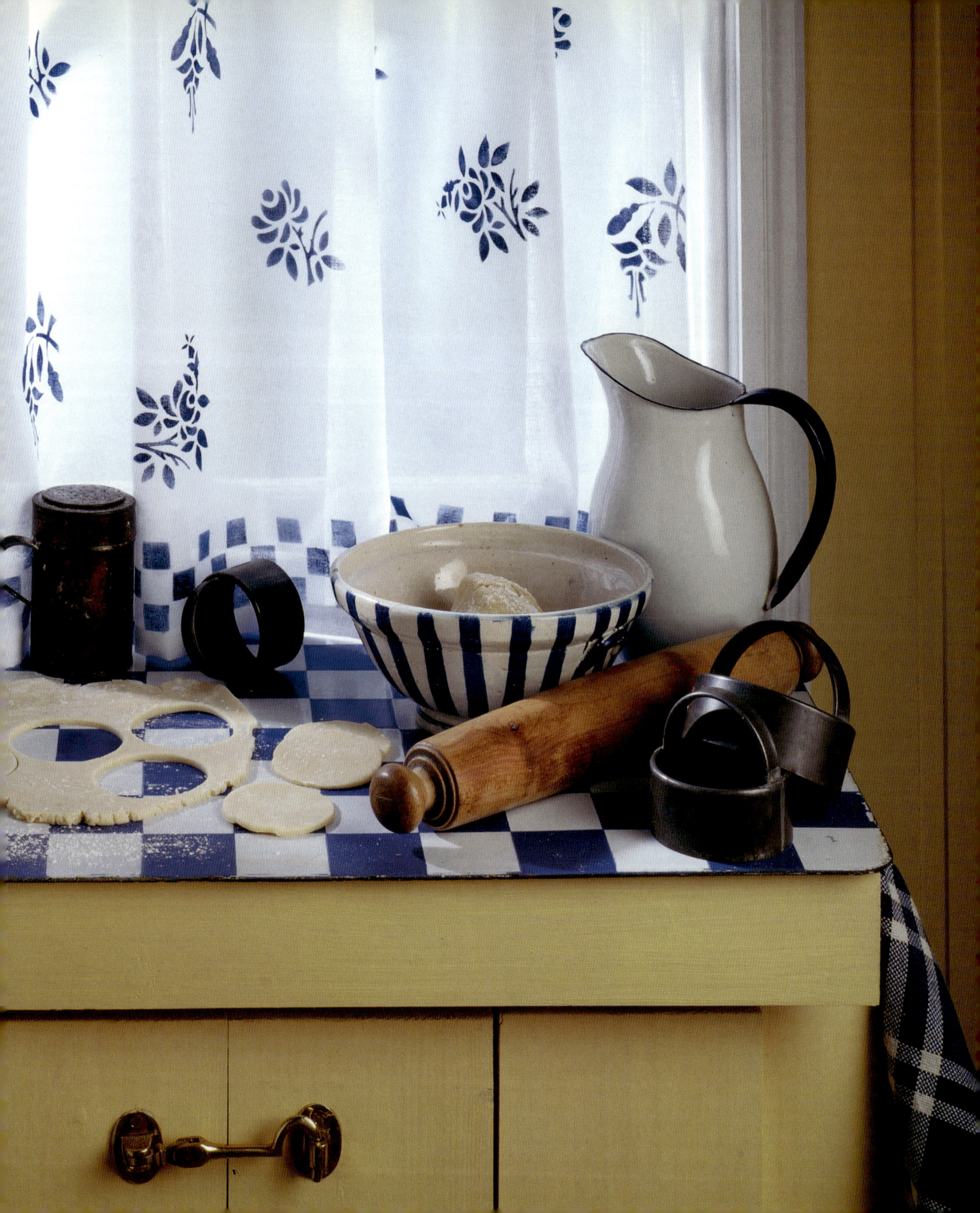

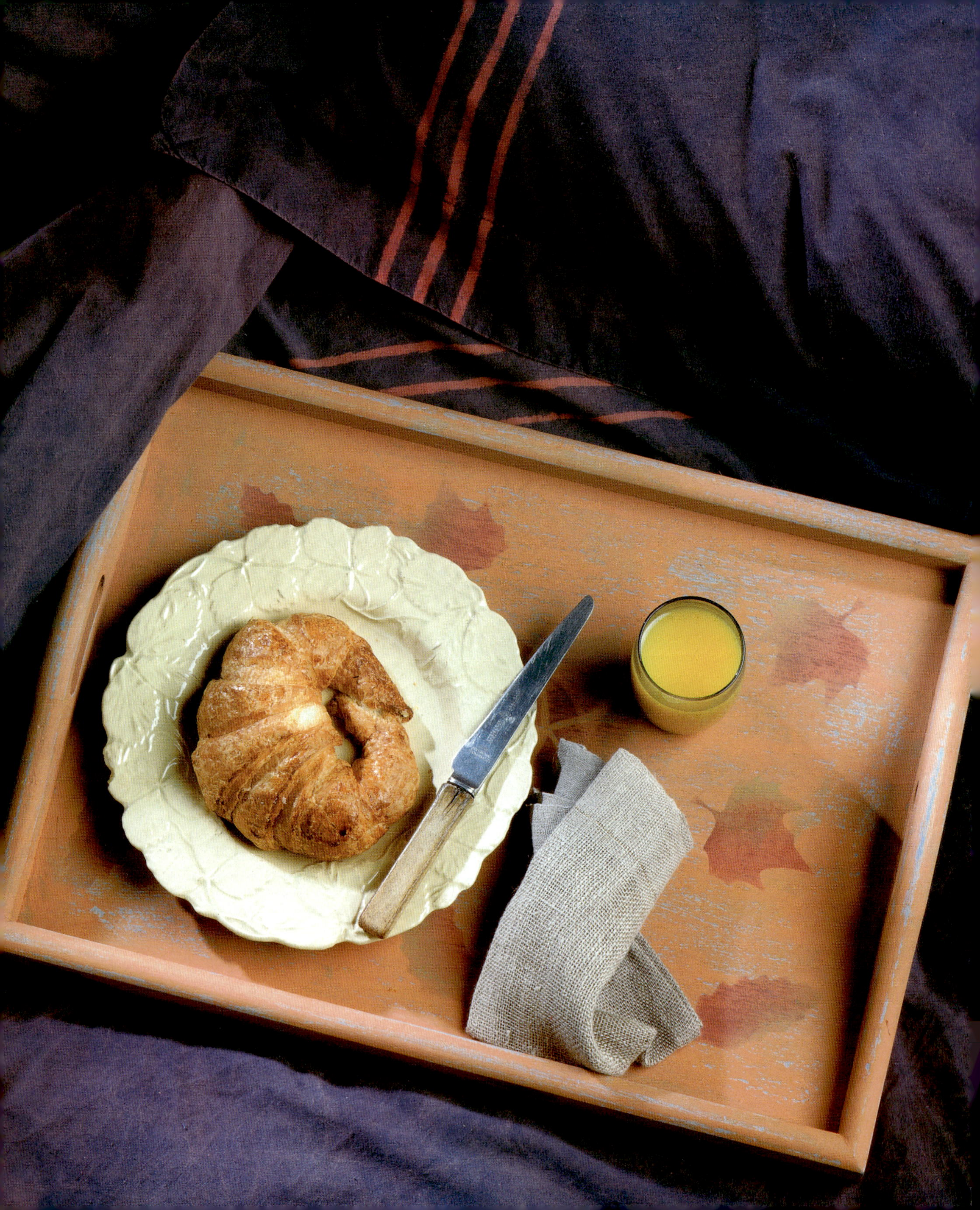

STENCILING

TRAY OF AUTUMN LEAVES

The rich colors of autumn leaves are captured here on a simple wood tray. Stick to warm, natural paint colors to suit the country style and simple lines of the tray. Use the templates provided here or draw around your own pressed leaves.

YOU WILL NEED
wooden tray
fine-grade sandpaper
water-based primer (if bare wood)
paintbrushes
latex paints in blue-gray and ocher
household candle
cloth
stencil cardboard
craft knife and cutting mat
spray adhesive
stencil brush
stencil paints in rust and terra-cotta
saucer
matte acrylic varnish

1 Sand the tray with fine-grade sandpaper to ensure a smooth surface. If the wood is bare, paint with a water-based primer. Apply two coats of blue-gray paint, letting it dry between coats.

2 Rub the candle over the edges of the tray and over the base until there is a build-up of wax. Think about which areas of the tray would become worn naturally and apply wax there.

3 Wipe away any loose bits of wax. Paint the whole tray with the ocher paint and let dry completely.

TRAY OF AUTUMN LEAVES

4 Lightly rub the tray with sandpaper to reveal some of the blue-gray paint underneath.

5 Trace the templates at the back of the book or draw around leaves. Cut out the stencils from stencil cardboard as described in the basic techniques.

Above: Building up layers of paint and rubbing back the top layer in places gives the tray a pleasing distressed look.

6 Lightly spray the back of the stencils with adhesive. Arrange the stencils on the tray and smooth down. Dip the stencil brush into the rust stencil paint and rub it on a saucer or cloth so that the brush is almost dry. Using circular movements, apply the color evenly over the stencils, working more on one side of each motif. Apply terra-cotta paint to the other side of the leaves to create shadow. Continue stenciling all over the tray. To give the tray a tough finish, apply two or three coats of varnish, letting each coat dry before applying the next.

STENCILING

GILDED CANDLES

Plain church candles look extra special when adorned with simple gold stars and stripes. Always associated with Christmas, candles are popular all year round for their soft romantic lighting. Cutting the stencils may be tricky, but it will take just minutes to spray on the gold paint.

YOU WILL NEED
acetate
selection of candles
felt-tip marker
craft knife and cutting mat
spray adhesive
masking tape
metallic spray paint

1 Wrap a piece of acetate around the candle. Do not overlap the edges. Mark and cut the acetate a fraction of an inch shorter than the candle.

2 Trace the star templates at the back of the book. Lay the piece of acetate over the stars and trace over them with a marker.

3 Cut out the stars using a craft knife and cutting mat. Be careful not to tear the acetate.

4 Spray one side of the stencil with adhesive and wrap it around the candle, centering it so that there is a small gap at either end. Secure the acetate seam with masking tape. Cover the top of the candle with tape, making sure there are no gaps.

GILDED CANDLES

5 Spray a fine mist of metallic spray paint over the candle, holding the can about 12 inches from the surface. If too much paint is applied, it will drip underneath the stencil. Keep checking that the stencil is carefully stuck down to avoid any fuzzy lines around the stars. Let the paint dry for a couple of minutes, then carefully remove the masking tape and acetate.

6 For a stars and stripes candle, cut strips of acetate and trace a line of small stars along each strip. Cut out with a craft knife as before. Spray one side of the acetate strips with adhesive. Stick the strips onto the candle, measuring the gaps in between to ensure equal spacing. Secure them with small pieces of masking tape at the seams.

7 Tape the top of the candle as before. Spray the candle with metallic paint and remove the masking tape and stencil when dry.

8 For a reverse stencil design, cut out individual star shapes from acetate. Apply spray adhesive to one side, stick onto the candle and mask the top of the candle as before. Spray with metallic paint and carefully remove the acetate stars when the paint is dry.

Above: A basketful of starry gilded candles makes a pretty gift.

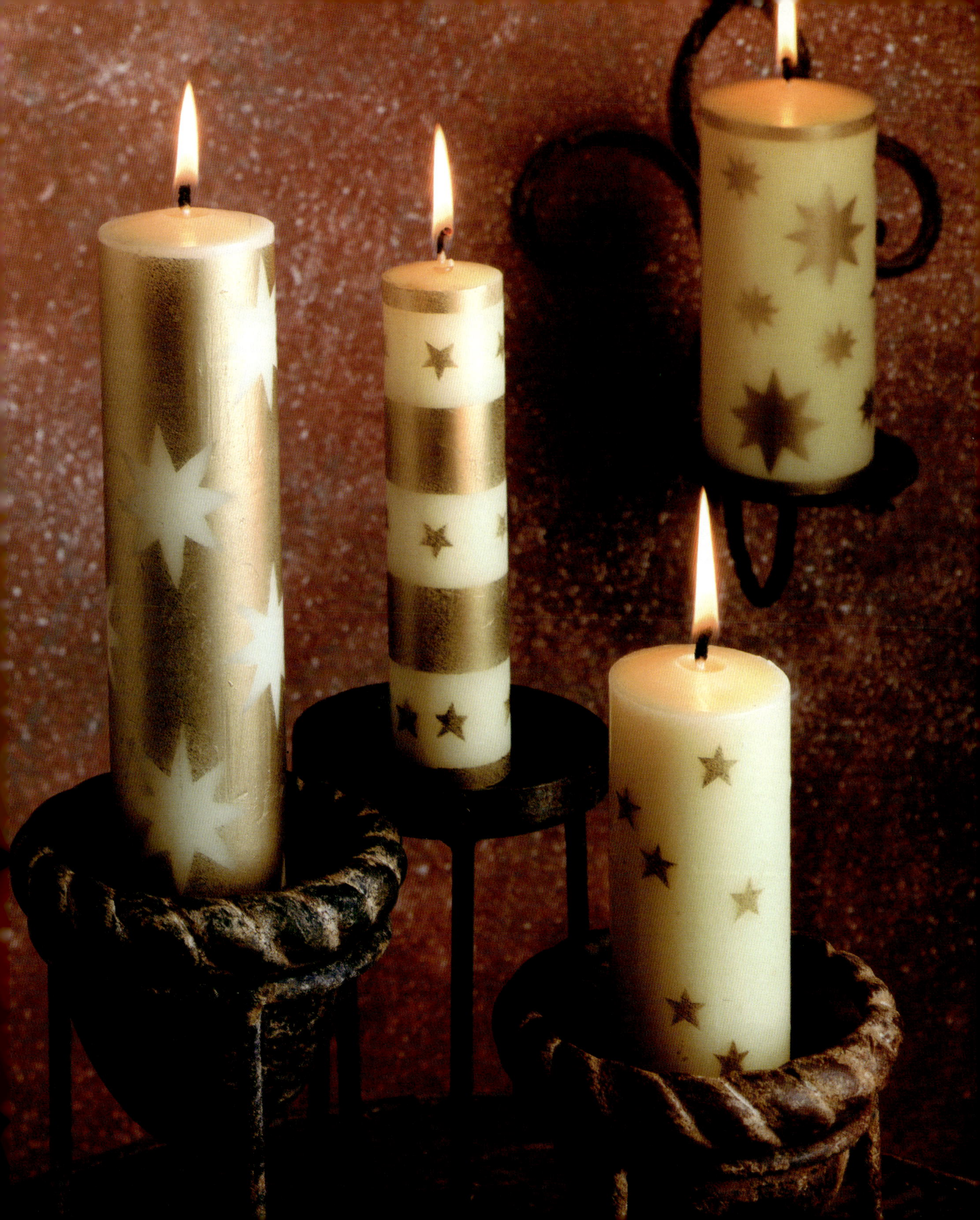

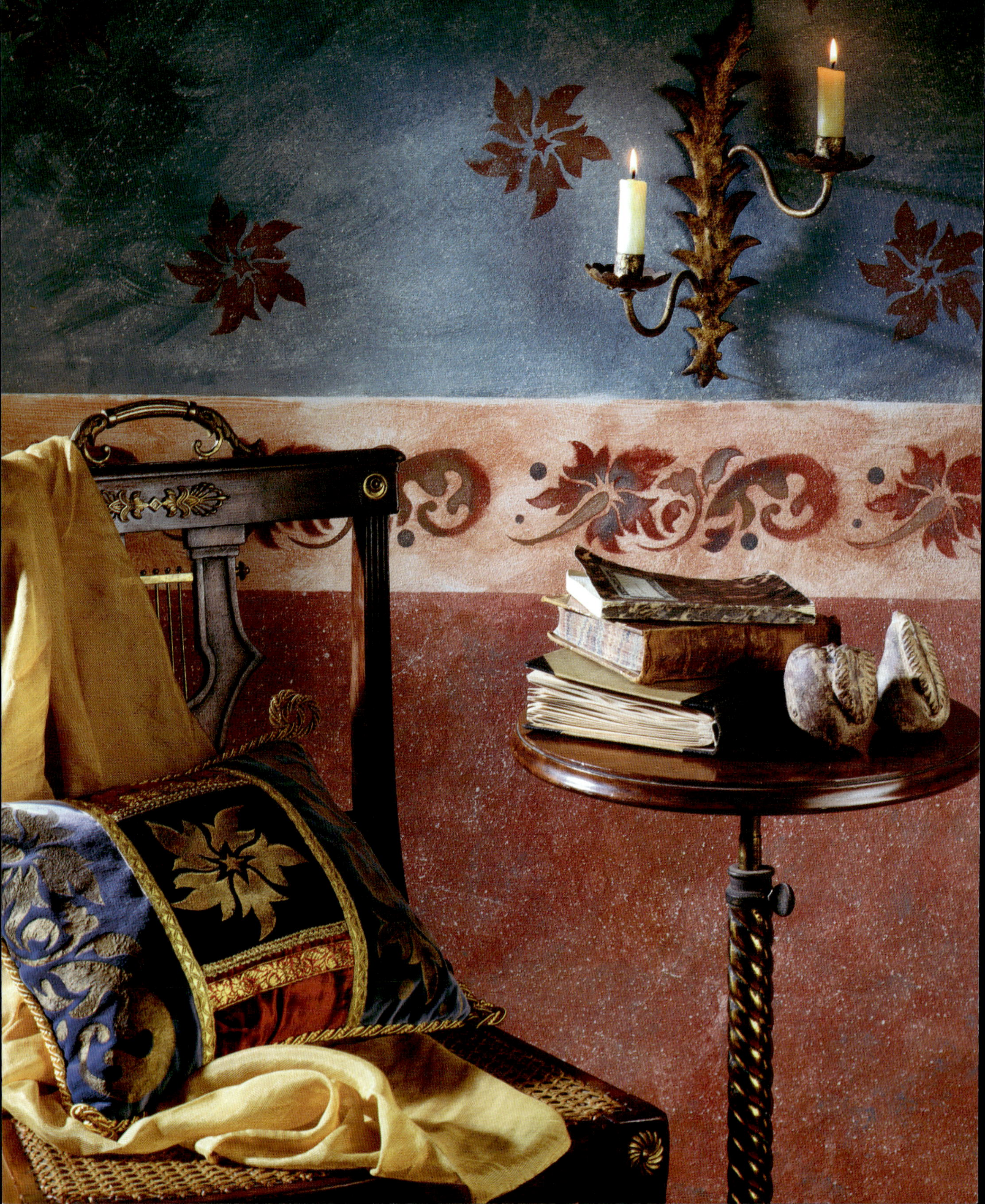

STENCILING

RENAISSANCE ART

Turn your hallway into a dramatic entrance with ornate stencils and rich colors. Combine them with gold accessories, velvets and braids to complete the theatrical setting. This design would also be ideal for creating an intimate dining room for candlelit dinners.

YOU WILL NEED
ruler
level
pencil
masking tape
latex paints in pale slate blue, terra-cotta
and pale peach
sponges
stencil brushes
stencil cardboard
craft knife and cutting mat
stencil paints in dark gray-blue, terra-cotta,
emerald and turquoise

1 Using a ruler and level, divide the wall in half horizontally with a pencil line, then draw a second line 6 inches above the first. Stick a line of masking tape just below this top line. Dilute one part slate blue latex with one part water and color the top half of the wall using a sponge.

2 Stick masking tape just above the bottom pencil line. Dilute terra-cotta latex with water and sponge over the lower half of the wall.

3 Sponge lightly over the terra-cotta with slate blue to add a textural effect. Remove the strips of masking tape.

4 Color the center band with diluted peach latex using a stencil brush. Trace the templates at the back of the book and cut out the stencils from stencil cardboard.

5 Stencil the wall motifs at roughly regular intervals over the upper part of the wall, using dark gray-blue. Rotate the stencil with every alternate motif to give movement to the design.

6 Starting at the right-hand side of the peach band, stencil the border motif with terra-cotta stencil paint. Add details in emerald and turquoise. Continue along the wall, positioning the stencil beside the previous motif so that the spaces are equal.

Right: Make a matching patchwork cushion cover with pieces of fabric stenciled with gold fabric paint. Add scraps of velvet and cover all the seams with ornate trimmings.

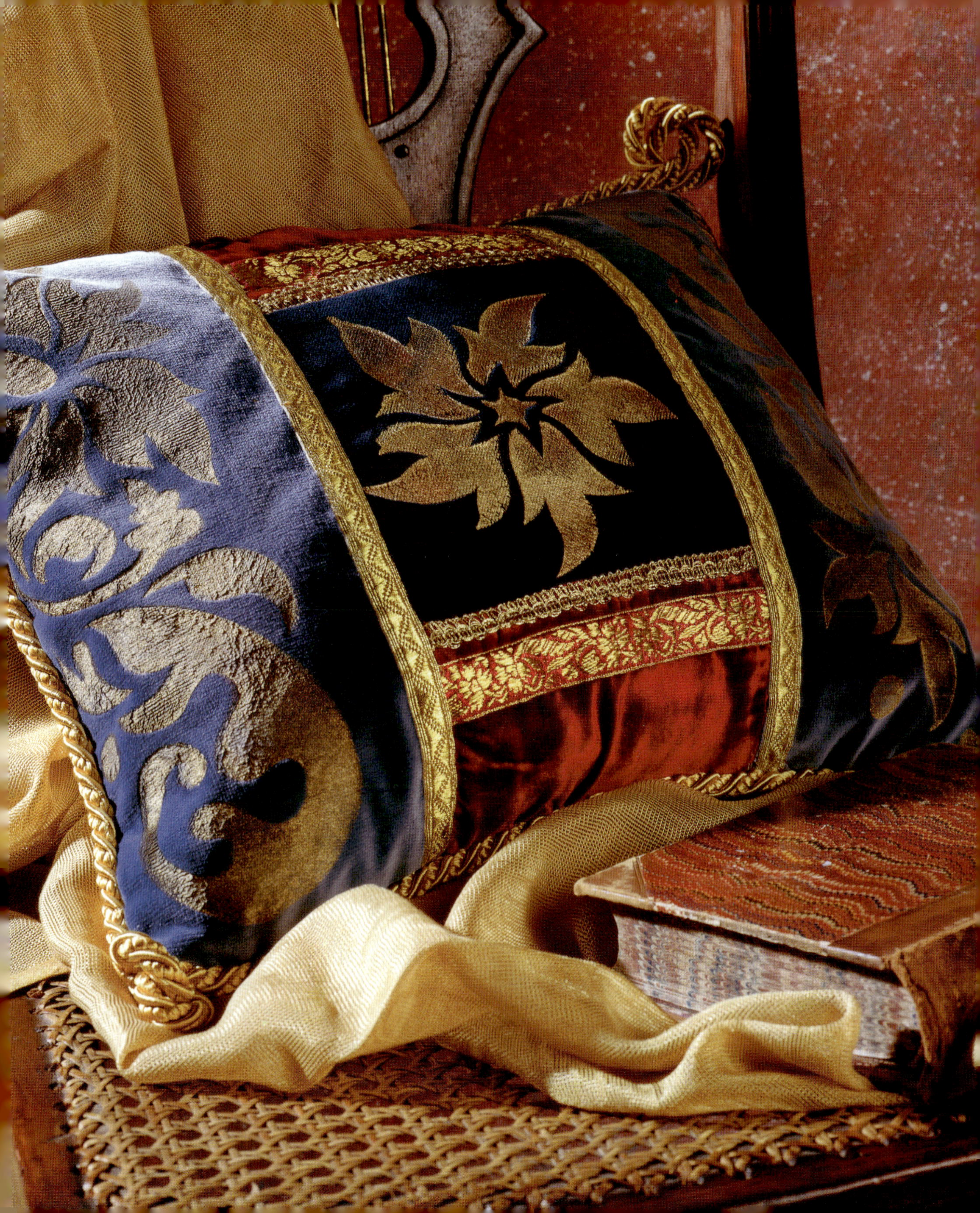

STENCILING

GEOMETRIC FLOOR TILES

This repeating pattern is derived from an ancient Greek mosaic floor. Cork floor tiles take color well—only use a small amount of paint and build it up in layers if necessary. Make two stencils, one for each color, so that the colors do not get mixed up.

YOU WILL NEED
graph paper
ruler
pencil
compass
stencil cardboard
craft knife and cutting mat
masking tape
12-inch cork tiles
spray adhesive
stencil paints in terra-cotta and blue
stencil brushes
acrylic sealer

1 Enlarge the quarter-section template at the back of the book so that it will fit within a 6-inch square. Using graph paper will make the design more accurate. Measure the three squares and draw the curves with a compass. Rub over all the pencil lines on the back with a pencil.

2 Cut two 12-inch squares from stencil cardboard and draw four lines, from corner to corner and edge to edge, to divide each card into eight equal segments. For the first stencil, tape the paper face up to one corner of the first piece of cardboard and draw around the corner and center square to transfer the design to the cardboard. Repeat on each corner, turning the paper 90° each time. Cut out the five squares. For the second stencil, draw along the curves and around the remaining square. Cut out these eight shapes.

GEOMETRIC FLOOR TILES

3 Wipe the tile to remove any cork dust and coat the back of the first stencil with spray adhesive. Stencil the squares using terra-cotta stencil paint and a stencil brush.

4 Let dry, then use the second stencil and blue paint to complete the design. Stencil the remaining tiles in the same way.

5 When all the tiles are complete, spray with acrylic sealer to make them waterproof. Attach them to the floor following the manufacturer's instructions.

Above: Make half the tiles in different colors for a checkerboard-patterned floor.

49

GEOMETRIC FLOOR TILES

Right: A gentle shading of blue has been added to the yellow shapes and yellow to the blue shapes to give a softer outline to the design.

Right: Different color combinations create very different effects. When using more than two colors, you will either need to cut more stencils or to mask the area that will be colored differently.

50

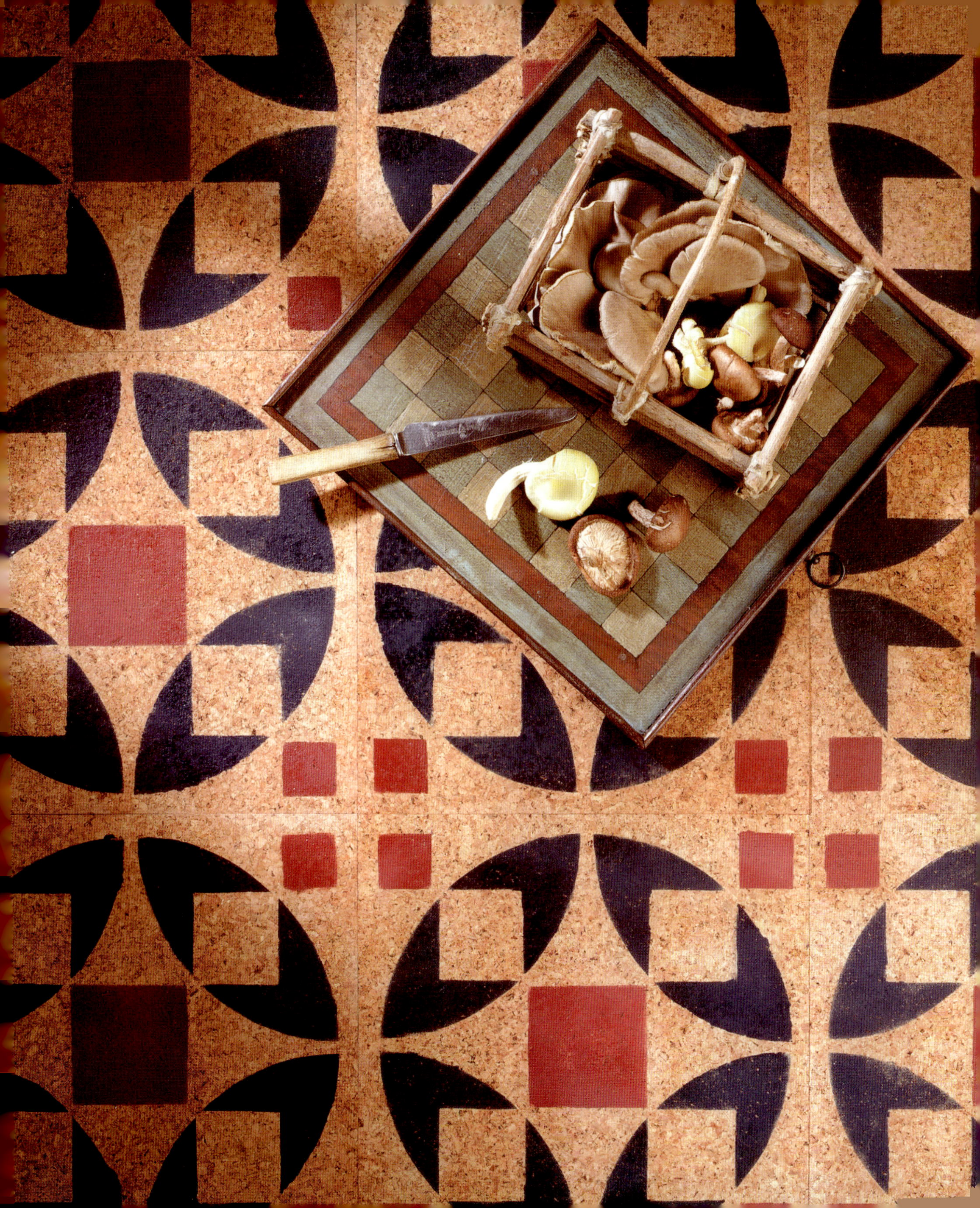

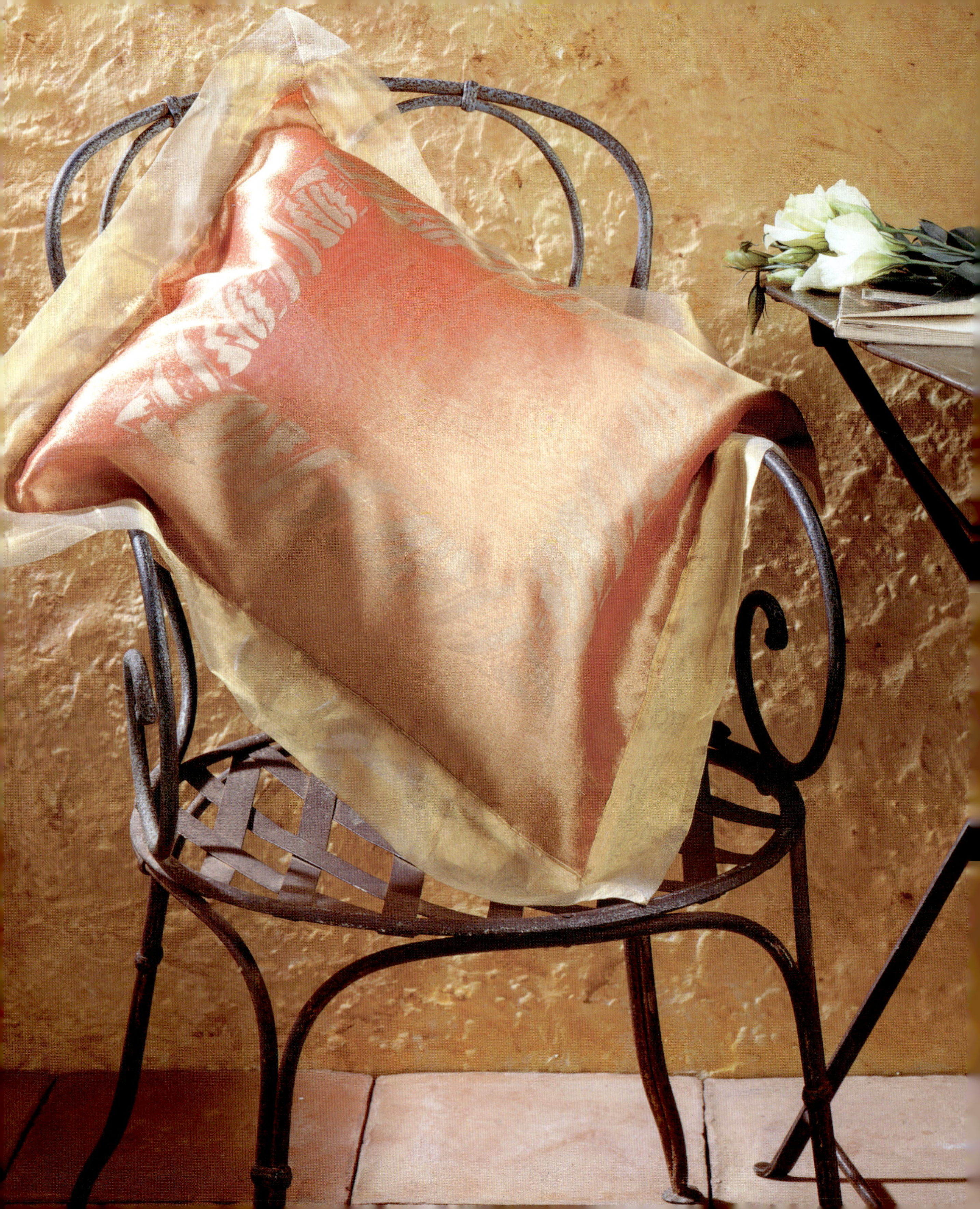

STENCILING

ORGANZA CUSHION

If you always thought stenciling had a simple, country look, then think again. This stunning organza cushion with gold stenciling takes the craft into the luxury class. Use the sharpest dressmaker's pins when handling organza to avoid marking the fabric.

YOU WILL NEED
dressmaker's graph paper
ruler
pencil
scissors
dressmaker's pins
organza, 1⅛ yard each in main color and contrasting color
stencil cardboard
craft knife and cutting mat
spray adhesive
scrap paper
masking tape
gold spray paint
needle and thread
sewing machine
iron
20-inch cushion pad

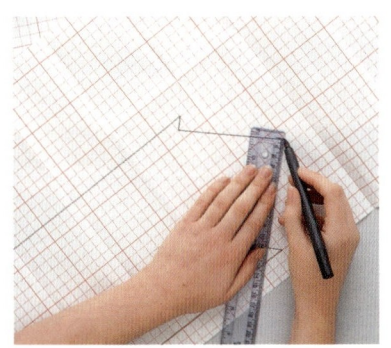

1 Copy the border template at the back of the book onto dressmaker's graph paper and cut it out. In addition, cut out a 21-inch square and a 21 x 16-inch rectangle from the graph paper.

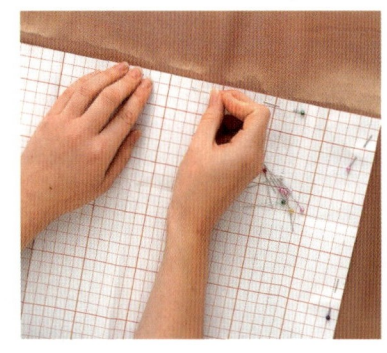

2 Pin the square and rectangle to the main color of organza. Cut two 21-inch squares and two rectangles measuring 21 x 16 inches from the main fabric. Cut four border pieces from the contrasting fabric.

3 Cut a 7 x 21-inch piece of stencil cardboard. Trace the template and transfer to the cardboard 3 inches from the bottom edge and with 2½ inches to spare at each end. Cut out the stencil.

4 Spray the back of the stencil with adhesive and position along the edge of the main organza fabric square. Cut two 45° miters from stencil cardboard, spray with adhesive and press in place. Mask the surrounding areas with scrap paper.

ORGANZA CUSHION

5 Spray with gold paint. Let dry and spray again. Remove the masking paper and stencil. Place the stencil along the next edge, put the miters in place and continue as before. Stencil the remaining two sides. Hem one long edge of each fabric rectangle by folding over ⅜ inch, then ⅝ inch. Pin, baste and machine-stitch the hem, then press.

6 Lay the stenciled fabric square face down and the second square on top. Lay the two rectangles on top of these, overlapping the stitched edges so that the raw edges line up with the square pieces. Pin, baste and machine-stitch ⅜ inch from the raw edge. Trim seam allowance to ¼ inch. Pin, baste and stitch the border pieces together at the mitered corners ½ inch from the raw edges. Trim the corners and turn the right way out. Press. Continue until the border pieces make a ring.

7 Press one of the raw edges under by ½ inch. Lay the pressed edge of the border fabric along the edge of the main fabric square and pin, baste and stitch in place.

8 Turn the cushion over and pull the border over. Turn under the border's raw edge by ½ inch and pin in place along the front of the cushion. Baste and stitch in place. Press. Insert the cushion pad.

STENCILING

TABLECLOTH AND NAPKINS

Inspiration for stencil designs are all around you, waiting to be discovered. Cutlery and kitchen utensils are wonderful graphic shapes, ideal for stenciling. Arrange them as borders around the edge of a cloth or place them formally on each side of an imaginary place setting.

YOU WILL NEED
acetate
craft knife and cutting mat
plain cotton napkins
and tablecloth
fabric paints in various colors
stencil brush
fine artist's paintbrush
iron

1 Trace the cutlery, heart and utensils templates at the back of the book and cut the stencils from acetate. Lay one of the napkins on a flat surface. Plan your design and start to stencil around the edge of the napkin.

2 Stencil hearts in between the cutlery stencils. Using a fine artist's paintbrush, paint dots around the hem of the napkins.

3 With the stencil brush, stencil hearts on the handles of some of the cutlery.

4 Stencil each napkin with a different pattern, varying the arrangement of the stencils.

5 Lay the tablecloth on a flat surface and begin to stencil the border of cutlery and hearts.

TABLECLOTH AND NAPKINS

6 Stencil the larger utensil shapes in the middle of the tablecloth. Stencil the handles first. Paint the tops of the utensils (for example, the whisk) in a contrasting color.

7 Stencil the slotted spoons and then fill in the holes in a different color.

8 Fill in the areas around the utensils with more cutlery stencils. Let the fabric paint dry and then iron the reverse of the fabric to set the paint.

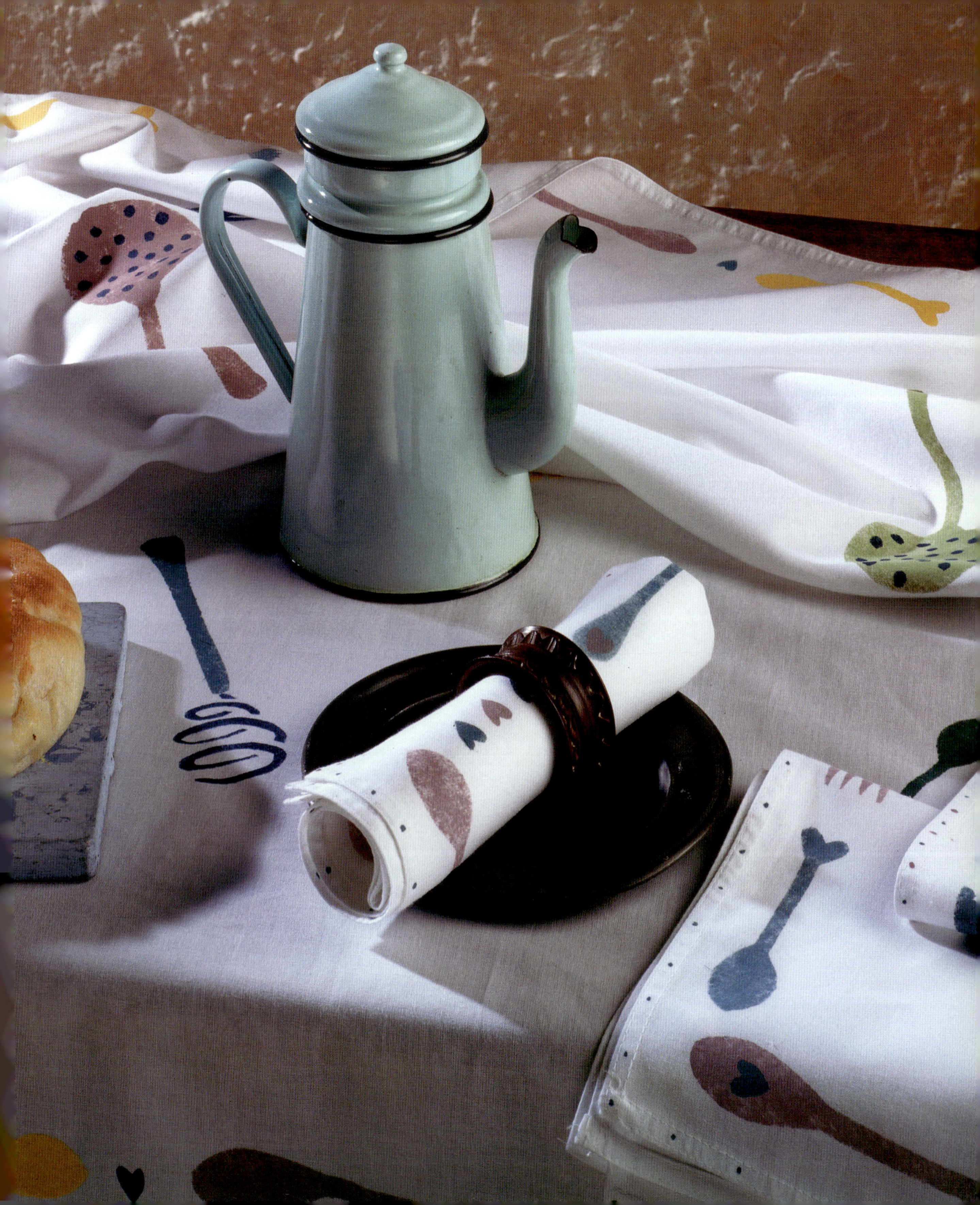

STENCILING

THROUGH THE GRAPEVINE

This classic grape stencil will bring back vacation memories of sipping Greek wine under a canopy of vines. The stenciled grapes are all the more effective set against the purple and green dry-brushed walls. Practice your paint effects on small boards before tackling full-scale walls.

YOU WILL NEED
large paintbrush
latex paints in purple and green
pencil
ruler
level
acetate
craft knife and cutting mat
masking tape
stencil paint in purple and lilac
stencil brush
silver gilt cream
soft cloth

1 Dip the end of a large paintbrush in purple latex, scrape off the excess and apply to the wall, brushing in varying directions and not completely covering the wall. This process is known as dry-brushing.

2 Repeat the process with green latex, filling in some of the gaps.

3 Draw a horizontal pencil line at the desired height on the wall using a ruler and level.

4 Trace the grape stencil at the back of the book and cut out the stencil from acetate. Tape the stencil in place with its top edge on the pencil line. Apply purple stencil paint over the whole stencil.

5 Add lilac stencil paint at the bottom of each window in the stencil to create highlights.

6 Dip the stencil brush in the silver gilt cream, brush off any excess and brush over the design using an up and down movement.

7 Select a few leaf shapes from the stencil and mask them off. Position randomly over the wall and stencil in purple. Brush over with the gilt cream. (They are too small to require the lilac highlight.)

THROUGH THE GRAPEVINE

8 Let the stenciling dry overnight. With a soft cloth, buff the silver cream to a shine.

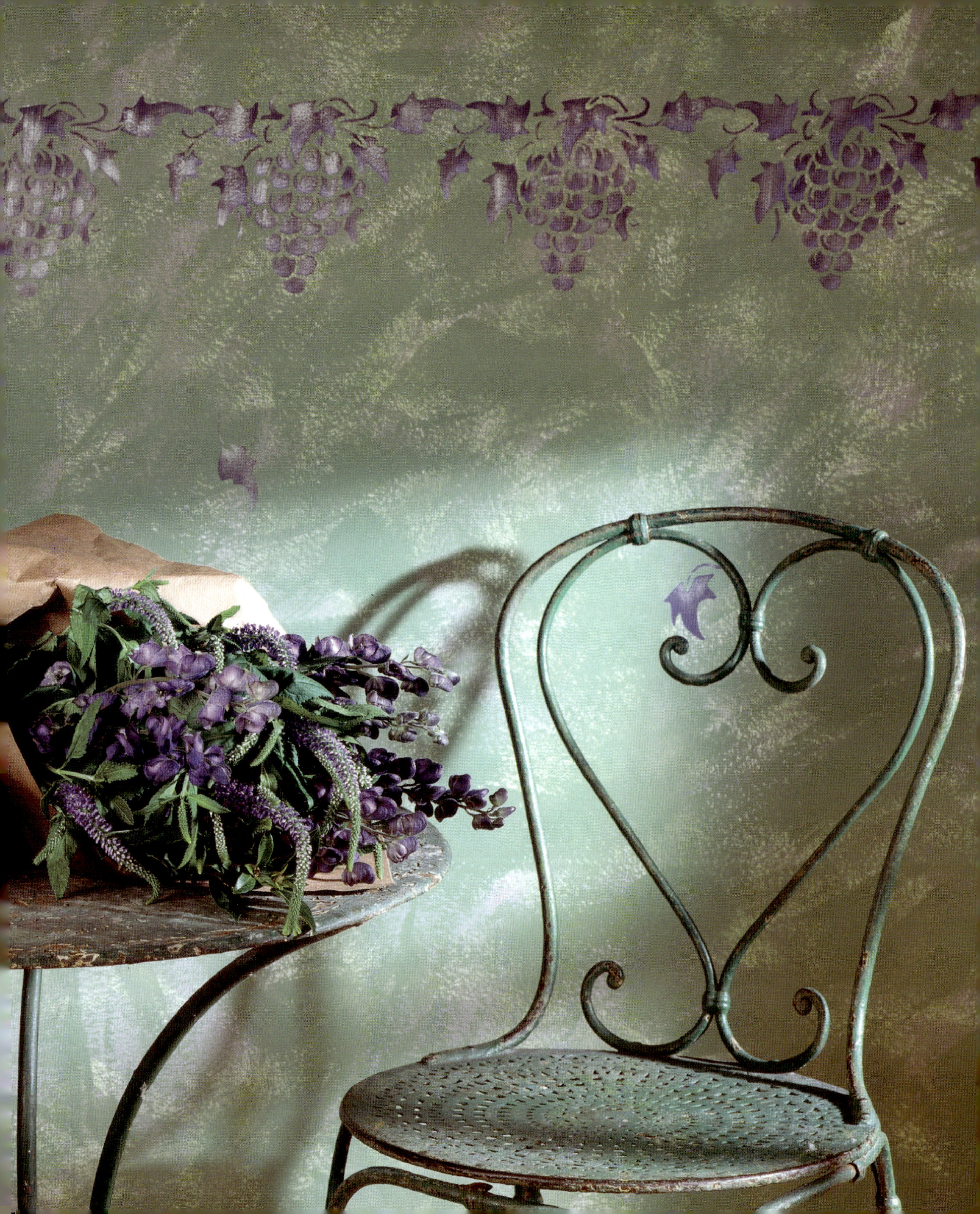

STENCILING

ROPE AND SHELLS

The chunky rope cleverly linking the seashells is echoed by individual stenciled knots. Shells are always popular motifs for a bathroom design and look good in many color combinations, from nautical blue and white to greens and aquas or pinks and corals.

YOU WILL NEED
large household sponges
latex paints in nautical blue and white
ruler
level
pencil
acetate
craft knife and cutting mat
masking tape
stencil paints in dark blue, light blue and camel
stencil brush
eraser
cloth

1 Using a household sponge, rub nautical blue latex paint over the wall to create a very rough and patchy finish. Let dry.

2 Using a clean sponge, rub a generous amount of white latex over the wall so that it almost covers the blue, giving a slightly mottled effect.

ROPE AND SHELLS

3 Using a ruler and level, draw a horizontal pencil line at the desired height of the border. Trace the seashore and knot templates at the back of the book and cut the stencils from acetate. Position the seashore stencil with its top edge on the pencil line and secure with masking tape. Stencil dark blue paint around the edges of the shells and seaweed, using a stencil brush.

4 Using light blue stencil paint, shade in the shells, the seaweed and the recesses of the rope.

5 Using the camel stencil paint, fill in the remainder of the rope and highlight the shells and seaweed. Continue to stencil the shell and rope border all the way around the room.

6 Draw a vertical line from each loop of rope to the baseboard. Starting 12 inches from the border, make pencil marks at 12-inch intervals down the line to mark the positions of the knots. Start every alternate line of marks 6 inches below the border so that the knots will be staggered.

ROPE AND SHELLS

7 Tape the knotted rope stencil onto the first pencil mark. Stencil dark blue in the recesses of the rope.

8 Stencil the remainder of the rope in camel. Let dry. Remove any visible pencil marks with an eraser and wipe with a slightly damp cloth.

Left: Create a variation on the sea theme by stenciling a row of starfish at chair-rail height.

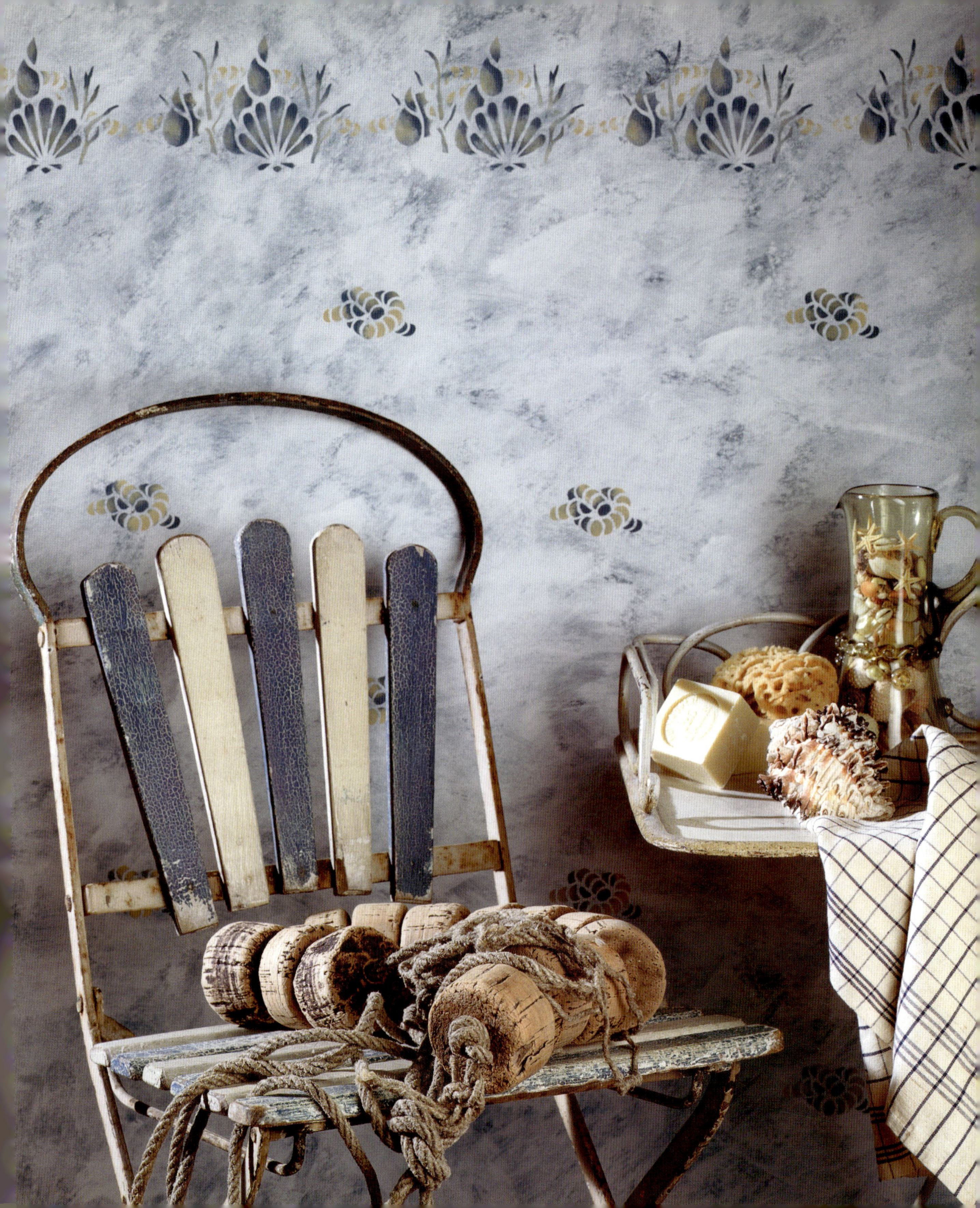

STENCILING

HERALDIC DINING ROOM

Lend an atmosphere of medieval luxury to your dining room with richly colored walls and heraldic motifs stenciled in the same deep tones. Gilt accessories, heavy fabrics and a profusion of candles coordinate well with this decor. All that remains is to prepare a sumptuous banquet.

YOU WILL NEED
large household sponges
latex paints in camel, deep red and deep purple
ruler
level
pencil
masking tape
acetate
craft knife and cutting mat
stencil brush
fine lining brush

1 Using a large household sponge, rub camel latex all over the wall. Let dry.

2 Repeat the process using a generous amount of deep red latex so that it almost covers the camel, giving a slightly mottled effect. Let dry.

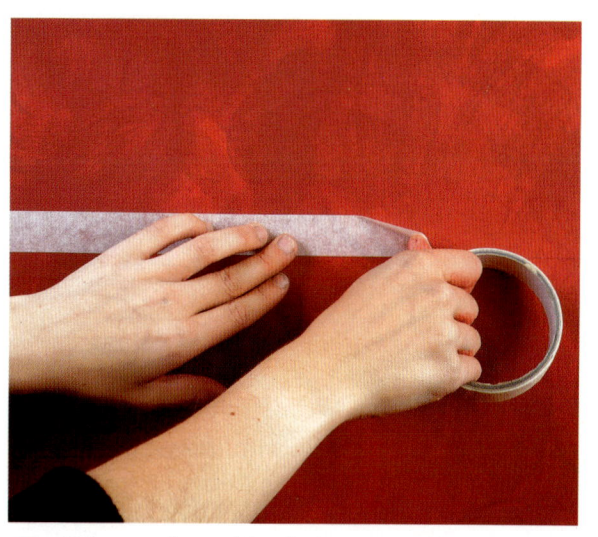

3 Using a ruler and level, draw a pencil line at chair-rail height and stick a line of masking tape just above it.

HERALDIC DINING ROOM

4 Sponge deep purple latex all over the wall below the masking tape to give a slightly mottled effect. Let dry, then remove the masking tape.

5 Trace the heraldic templates at the back of the book and cut out the stencils from acetate. Secure the rose stencil above the dividing line and stencil in purple latex, using the stencil brush. When dry, position the fleur-de-lis stencil next to the rose and stencil in camel latex. Continue to alternate the stencils around the room.

6 Place the highlighting stencils over the painted motifs and, with a stencil brush, add purple highlights to the camel fleurs-de-lis and camel highlights to the purple roses.

7 Flip the stencils over and position as mirror images below the previously stenciled motifs. Stencil the roses in camel and the fleurs-de-lis in red.

HERALDIC DINING ROOM

8 Add highlights as before, using camel on the fleurs-de-lis and purple on the camel roses.

9 Using a fine lining brush and camel paint, paint a narrow line where the red and purple paints meet. If you do not have the confidence to do this freehand, position two rows of masking tape on the wall, leaving a small gap in between. When the line of paint is dry, carefully remove the masking tape.

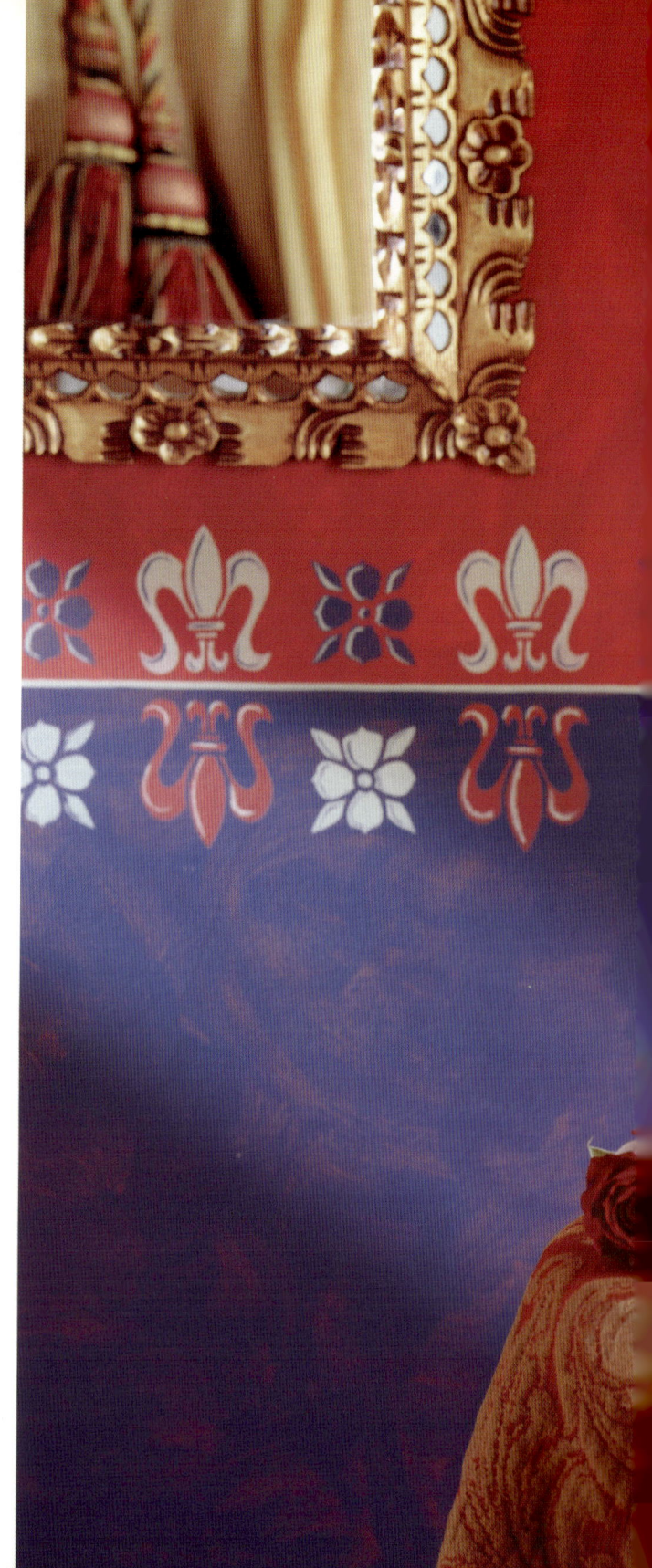

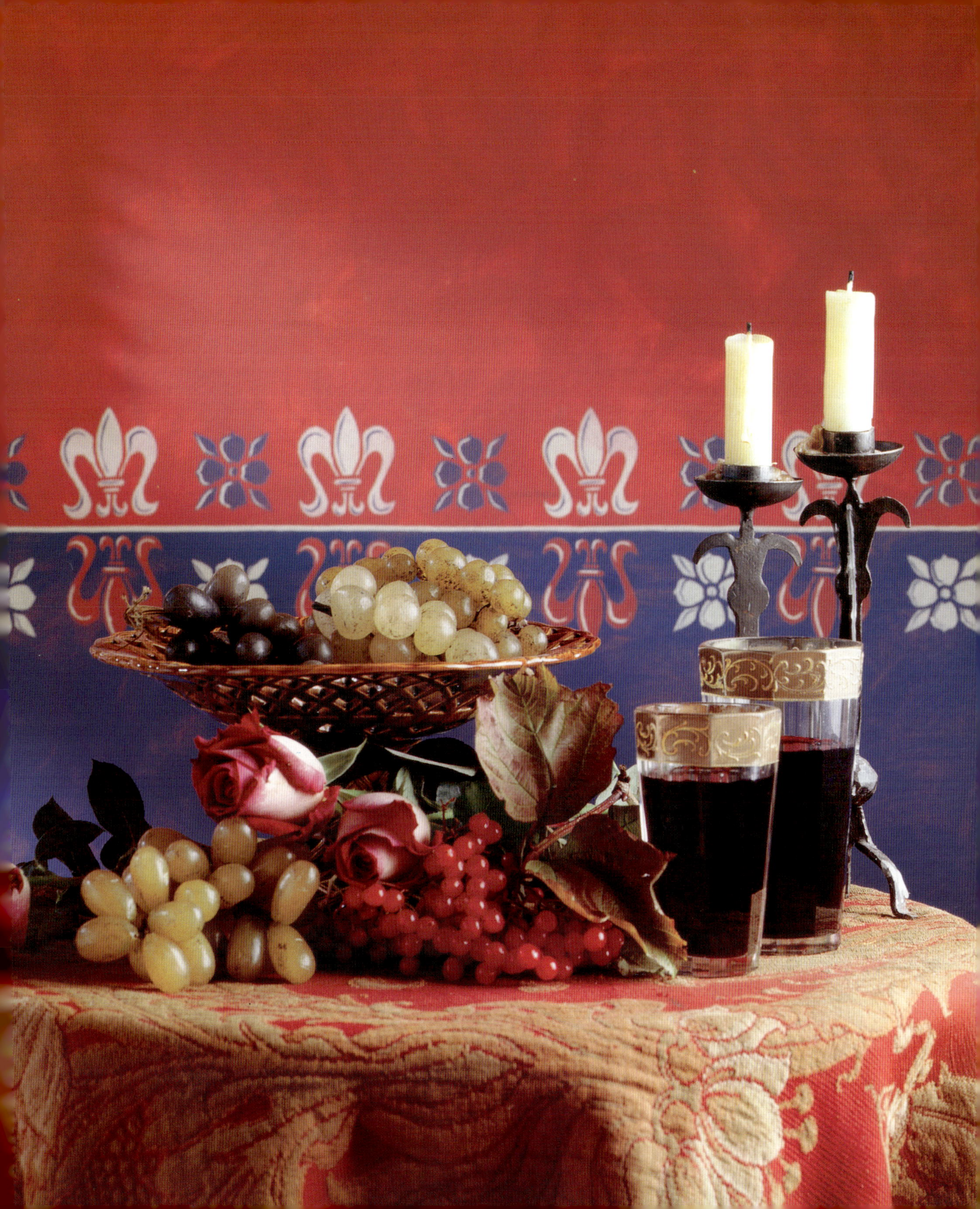

STENCILING

TROMPE L'ŒIL PLATES

A shelf full of decorative painted plates adds a fun touch to a kitchen corner. Follow these plate designs or translate your own patterned china into stencils to give a coordinated look. Why not add some individual plates to the wall as well?

YOU WILL NEED
stencil cardboard
pencil
ruler
craft knife and cutting mat
9-inch-diameter plate
compass
spray adhesive
newspaper or brown paper
masking tape
spray paints in white, cream, a range of pinks and mauves, light green, dark green, red, blue and gray

1 Cut three 12-inch square pieces of stencil cardboard. Mark the center of each piece of cardboard by finding the center of each edge and measuring a horizontal and vertical line across each square to connect the marks.

2 Draw a line 1¼ inch in from all four edges of each piece of cardboard. Place the plate in the center of the cardboard and draw around the edge. Cut out the plate shape from the first piece of stencil cardboard (stencil 1).

3 Using a compass, draw a circle about 1½ inches from the edge of the plate on the two remaining pieces of cardboard.

4 Trace or photocopy the plate template at the back of the book to the desired size and transfer it to the second piece of stencil cardboard.

70

TROMPE-L'ŒIL PLATES

5 Cut out the design with a craft knife on a cutting mat. Cut out the smaller areas first and the larger areas last (stencil 2). On the third piece of stencil cardboard, cut out the inner circle (stencil 3).

6 Draw a faint horizontal pencil line on the wall and put two marks 12 inches apart on the line to act as a guide for positioning the stencils. Spray the back of the plate stencil (1) with adhesive and place in position on the wall. Press down firmly to ensure good contact. Mask off the surrounding area with paper and masking tape, leaving no gaps. Spray white and cream spray paint onto the stencil. Remove the masks and stencil.

7 Attach the flower stencil (2) to the wall with spray adhesive, lining it up with the marks on the wall. Mask off the surrounding area. Stick small pieces of masking tape over the leaves on the stencil. Spray the flowers with pinks and mauves, applying a fine layer of paint in short, sharp puffs. Try each paint color on the mask surrounding the stencil to test the color and to make sure that the nozzle is clear.

8 Remove the masking tape from the leaves. Fold a small piece of cardboard in half and use it to shield the rest of the stencil from paint. Spray the leaves using light and dark green paints, trying not to get too much green on the flowers.

9 Cut a small hole in a piece of cardboard and use to spray the centers of the flowers green.

10 Hold the shield of cardboard around the dot designs on the border, and spray each one with red paint. Spray blue paint over the wavy lines on the border. Again, do not apply too much paint. Remove the masks and carefully remove the stencil. ▶

TROMPE-L'ŒIL PLATES

11 Spray the back of the last stencil (3) with adhesive and position on the wall. Mask off the surrounding area as before. Spray an extremely fine mist of gray paint over the top left-hand side and bottom right-hand side of the plate design to create a shadow. Aim the nozzle slightly away from the stencil to ensure that hardly any paint hits the wall. Remove the masks and stencil.

12 Reposition stencil 1 on the wall and spray a very fine mist of blue paint around the edge of the plate. Repeat all stages along the edge of the shelf length.

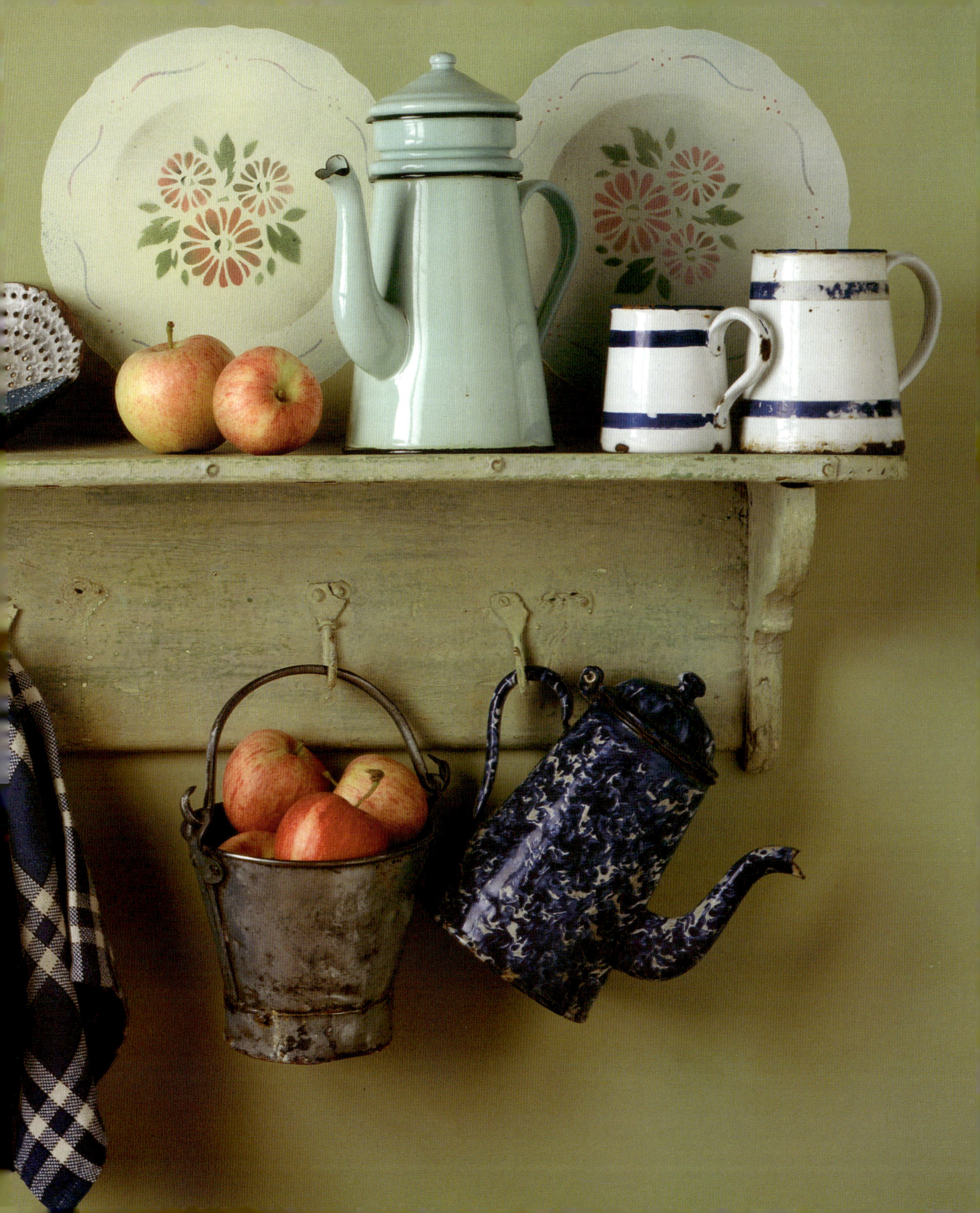

STENCILING

CELESTIAL CHERUBS

This exuberant baroque decoration is perfect for a sumptuous bedroom. The cherubs are stenciled in metallic shades of bronze, gold and copper, but you could use plain colors for a simpler result that would be suitable for a child's room.

YOU WILL NEED
latex paints in white, blue and gray
paintbrush
sponge
stencil cardboard
craft knife and cutting mat
masking tape
stencil paints in gold, copper, bronze and white
stencil brush

1 Paint the wall with white latex. Next, dilute one part blue latex with one part water and, using a sponge, lightly apply it to the wall.

2 Sponge in a few areas of gray to give the impression of a cloudy sky. Sponge in a few pale areas by mixing a little white into the gray paint to suggest the edges of clouds.

3 Trace the cherub and heart templates at the back of the book and cut out the stencils from stencil cardboard. Secure the cherub stencil to the wall with masking tape. Stencil the body of the cherub in gold.

4 Stencil the wings and bow in copper, covering the adjacent parts of the stencil with scrap paper.

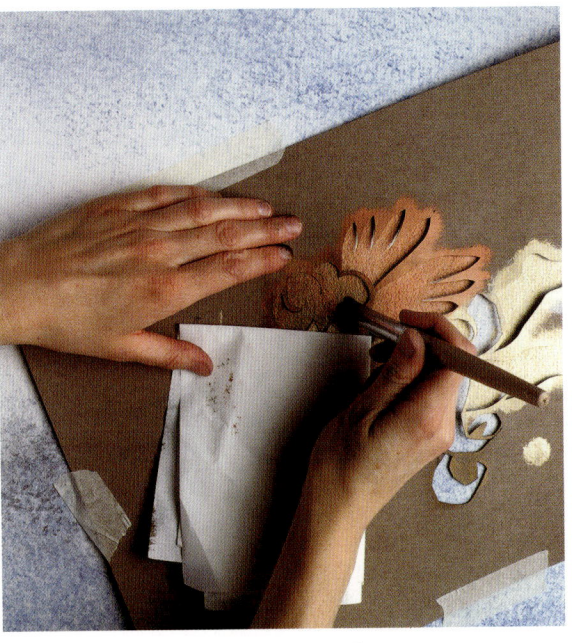

5 Stencil the hair and arrow in bronze.

6 Stencil the drape in white with some bronze shadows.

CELESTIAL CHERUBS

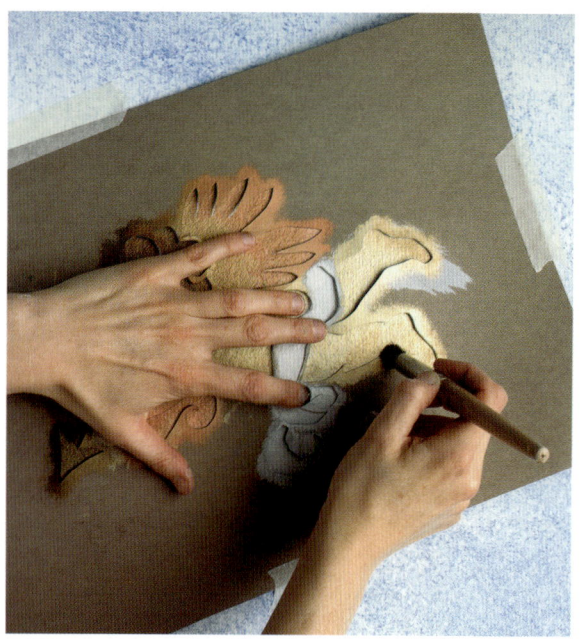

7 To give a three-dimensional effect to the whole design, add bronze shadows at the edges of the various parts of the motif.

8 Stencil more cherubs, varying the design by reversing the cardboard occasionally. Stencil the interlinked hearts in the spaces using bronze paint.

Right: Try to position the stencils so that the cupids are aiming their arrows at the interlinked hearts – perfect for a romantic bedroom.

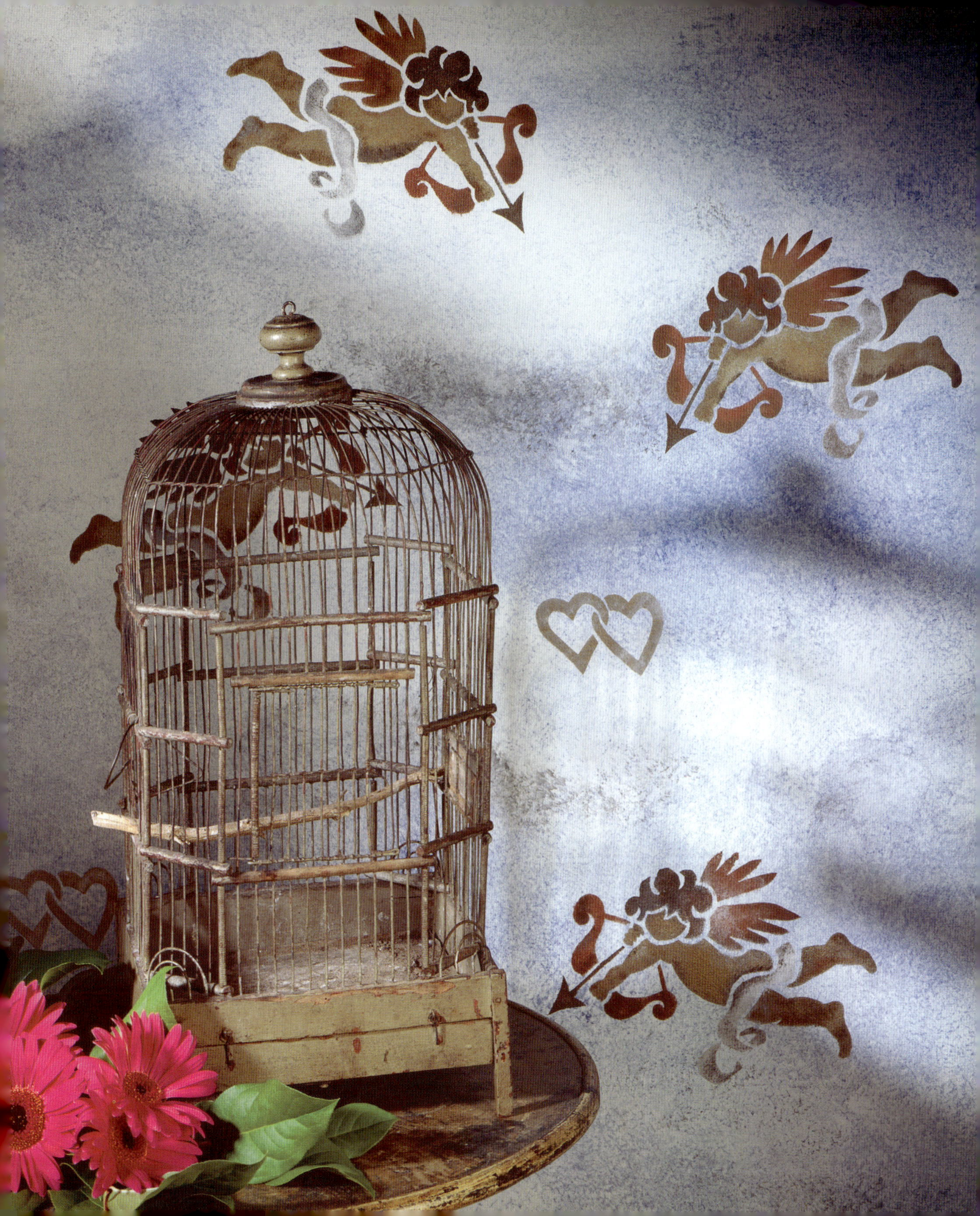

STENCILING

MATERIALS

A variety of materials can be used for stenciling, from special stenciling paints and sticks to acrylics and latex. Each has its own properties and will create different effects.

ACRYLIC STENCIL PAINT
Acrylic stencil paint is quick-drying, reducing the possibility of the paint running and seeping behind the stencil. Acrylic stencil paints are available in a wide range of colors, and can be mixed for more subtle shades.

ACRYLIC VARNISH
This is useful for sealing finished projects.

FABRIC PAINT
This is used in the same way as acrylic stencil paint, and comes in an equally wide range of colors. Set with an iron according to the manufacturer's instructions, it will withstand washing and everyday use. As with ordinary stencil paint, do not overload the brush with color, as it will seep into the fabric. Always back the fabric you are stenciling with scrap paper or newspaper to prevent the paint from marking the work surface.

GOLD LEAF AND GOLD SIZE
These can be used to great effect. The actual design is stenciled with gold size. The size is then left to become tacky, and the gold leaf is rubbed over the design.

LATEX PAINT
Ordinary household latex can also be used for stenciling. It is best to avoid the cheaper varieties, as these contain a lot of water and will seep through the stencil.

METALLIC CREAMS
These are available in many different metallic finishes, from gold to copper, bronze and silver. Apply as highlights on a painted base, or use for the entire design. Creams can be applied with cloths or your fingertip.

OIL-BASED STENCIL STICKS
AND CREAMS
The sticks can be used in the same way as a wax crayon, while the creams can be applied with a brush or your fingertip. With either one, there is no danger of overloading the color, and they won't run. The disadvantage is their long drying time (overnight in some cases); also, the colors can become muddy when mixed. Sticks and creams are also available for fabrics.

Clockwise from top left: acrylic stencil paint, oil-based cream and metallic creams, fabric paint, oil-based stencil sticks, latex paint, gold leaf, acrylic varnish and gold size.

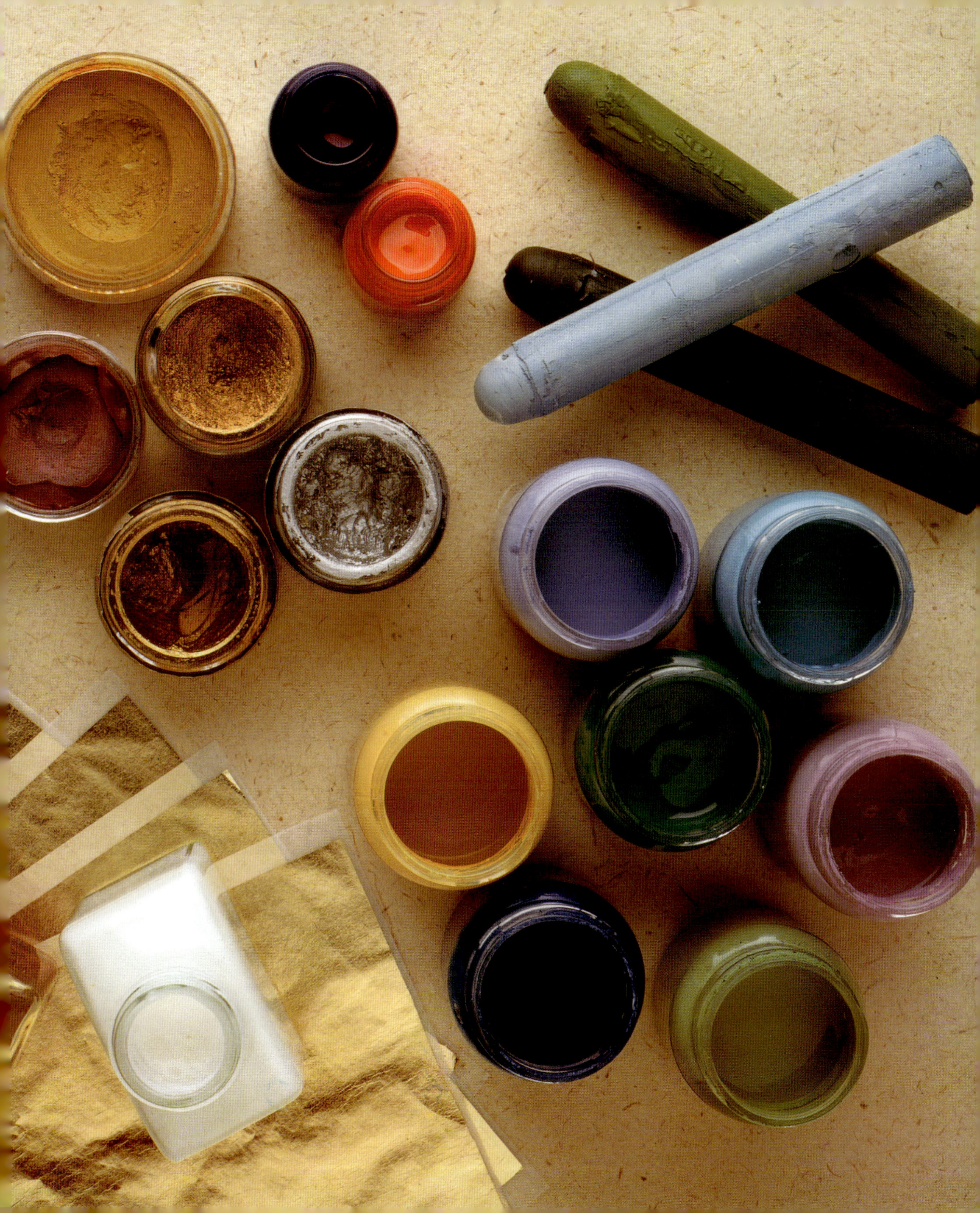

STENCILING

EQUIPMENT

Stenciling does not require a great deal of special equipment; many of the items used are commonly found in most households. A few tools, however, will make the job easier.

BRUSHES
It is worth investing in a set of good stencil brushes. The ends of the brushes should be flat and the bristles firm, to let you control the application of paint. A medium-size brush (1½-inch diameter) is a useful, all-purpose size, but you may want to buy one size smaller and one size larger as well. You will need a selection of household paintbrushes for applying large areas of background color, and small artist's paintbrushes for adding fine details.

CRAFT KNIFE
Use for cutting out stencils from cardboard.

CUTTING MAT
This provides a firm surface to cut into and will help prevent the craft knife from slipping.

MASKING TAPE
As the stencil may need to be repositioned, it is advisable to hold it in place with masking tape, which can be removed fairly easily from most surfaces.

PAINT-MIXING CONTAINER
This may be necessary for mixing paints and washes.

PENCILS
Keep a selection of soft and hard pencils to transfer the stencil design onto cardboard. Use an ordinary pencil to mark the positions of the stencils before applying.

STENCIL CARDBOARD
The material used to make the stencil is a matter of preference. Specialty stencil cardboard is available waxed, which means that it will last longer, but ordinary cardboard or heavy paper can also be used. It is worth purchasing a sheet of clear acetate if you wish to keep your stencil design, to reuse time and again.

TAPE MEASURE AND STRAIGHTEDGES
Some patterns may require accuracy. Measuring and planning the positions of your stencils before you begin will aid the result.

TRACING PAPER
Use to trace and transfer your stencil design onto stencil cardboard.

Clockwise from top left: straightedges, tape measure, stencil brushes, household paintbrush, cutting mat, stencil cardboard, tracing paper, pencil, craft knife, paint-mixing container, masking tape.

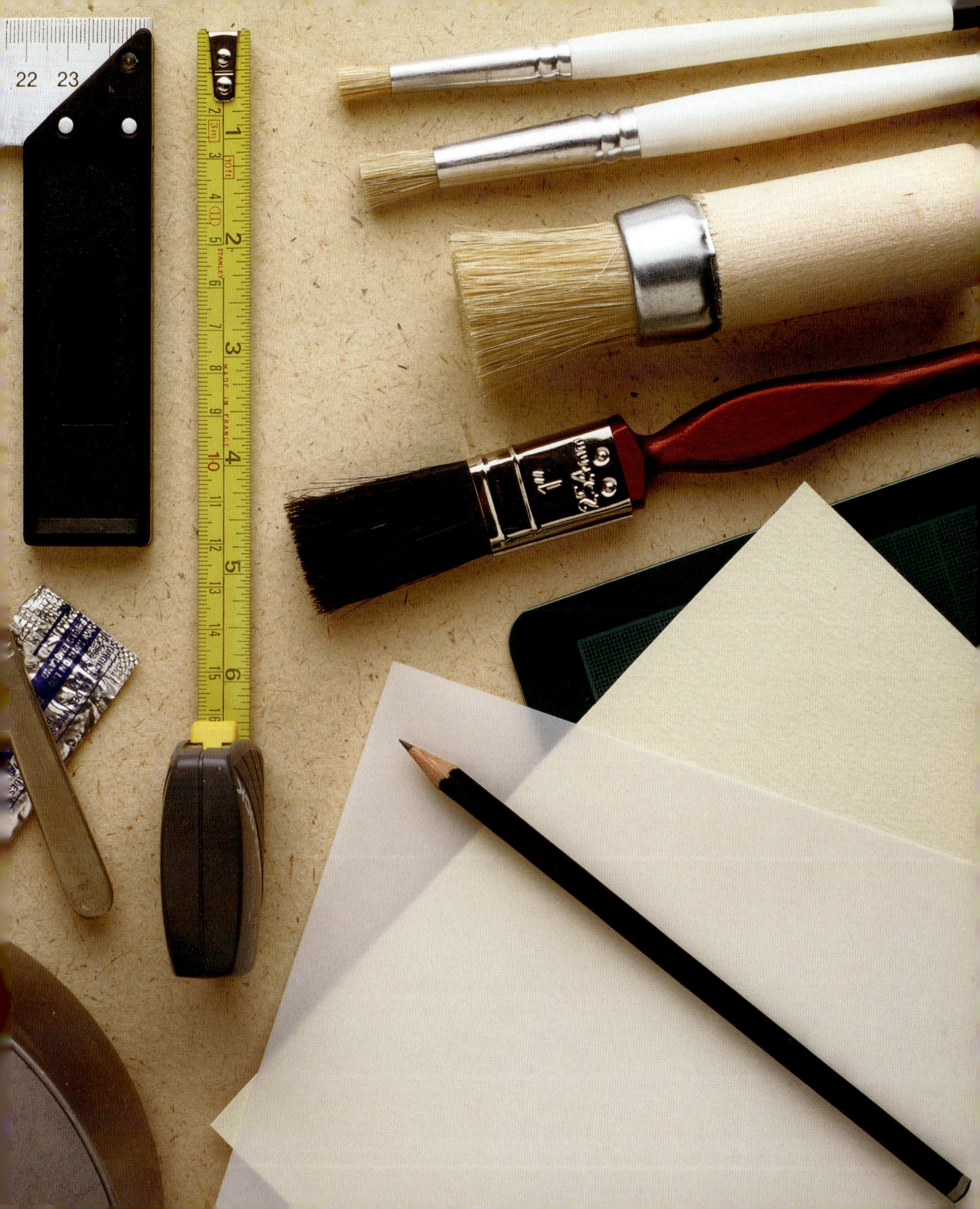

STANLEY
MADE IN FRANCE

STENCILING

BASIC TECHNIQUES

Stenciling is not difficult to master, but it is worth practicing on a small area to get used to handling the brush and to become accustomed to the properties of the paints you use. Some of the tips and techniques suggested below will make the task easier.

TRANSFERRING TEMPLATES

1 To transfer a template onto a piece of stencil cardboard, place a piece of tracing paper over the design, and draw over it with a hard pencil.

2 Turn over the tracing paper and, on the back of the design, rub over the lines you have drawn with a soft pencil.

3 Turn the tracing paper back to the right side and place on top of a sheet of stencil cardboard. Draw over the original lines with a hard pencil.

CUTTING STENCILS

1 Place the stencil on a cutting mat or piece of thick cardboard and tape in place. Use a craft knife for cutting.

2 It is safer to move the cutting mat toward you and the knife when working around awkward shapes. Continue, moving the mat.

BASIC TECHNIQUES

BLOCK STENCILING

Use for filling in large areas in a single, solid color. As in all stenciling, remember not to apply the paint too heavily – less is more. Always blot the paint onto a piece of cardboard before you begin.

BLOCK STENCILING WITH SECOND COLOR STIPPLED

When applying two colors, always apply the lighter shade first, then the darker. Do not cover the entire surface with the first color; leave a gap for the second shade, then blend later. Use a separate, clean brush for each color.

TWO-COLOR BLOCKING

When you apply the first color, do not fully block out the petals; instead, outline them with the first color and leave the centers bare. Use the second color to fill. Take care not to apply your paint too heavily.

ROTATED FLOWER WITH BLOCKED LEAVES

Using a very dry brush with a tiny amount of paint, rotate the bristles in a circular motion. This rotating action leaves enough paint on the surface for a lighter, softer look than a block application. Use the same effect in a darker color on the inside of the petals.

ROTATING AND SHADING

Using a very dry brush with a tiny amount of paint, place your brush on one side of the stencil and rotate the brush in circles. Repeat, using a slightly darker color on the edges, for soft shading.

ROTATING AND SHADING IN TWO COLORS

This is similar to rotating and shading, but is more directional. Using a very dry brush with a tiny amount of paint, place your brush in the center of the flower and rotate the bristles slightly outward. Repeat, using a slightly darker color.

STENCILING

Rotating brush with leaves flicked

Fill in the petals by rotating a very dry brush and a tiny amount of paint. For the flicking effect on the leaves, use slightly more paint on the brush. Working from the center, flick the paint outward once or twice. Do not overdo.

Dry-brushing, rotating from edge

Using big circular strokes, work from the outside of the whole stencil, moving inward. This should leave you with more paint on the outside, as there will be less and less paint on your brush as you move inward.

Brushing up and down from sides

This is similar to flicking. Using slightly more paint on your brush than you would for rotating, brush up and down, then from side to side. Keep your lines vertical and horizontal to give a lined effect.

Brushing up and down

Using slightly more paint on your brush than you would for rotating, brush up and down only, taking care to keep your lines vertical.

Dry-brushing with curve

Using the rotating technique, start at the center and work outward in big circles.

Dry-brushing and rotating

Apply a tiny amount of paint by rotating the bristles from the center and from the outside tips, to give more paint in these areas. Work along the line, using less pressure than on the center and the tips. This gives a softer effect on the areas in between.

BASIC TECHNIQUES

ROUGH STIPPLING

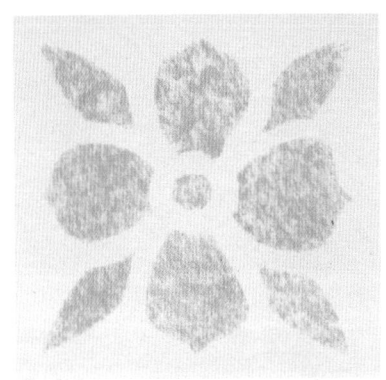

This method uses more paint and less pressure than rotating or flicking. Taking a reasonable amount of paint on the bristles of your brush, simply place it down lightly. This gives a rougher look. Do not go over it too many times, as this spoils the effect.

TWO-COLOR STIPPLING

Use less paint than for rough stippling. The second color is stippled out from the center, to blend.

ONE-SIDED STIPPLING

Apply the lighter color first, to a point just past the center. Apply the darker color, and stipple to the center. Always start on the outer edge so that you leave more paint on the edges of the stencil design.

DRY-BRUSH STIPPLING

This is similar to stippling, except that it is essential to dab most of the paint off the bristles before you start. This gives a softer stippling effect.

GENTLE STIPPLING FROM EDGE

Using a very dry brush (dab most of the paint off the bristles before you start), stipple from the outside, working inward. By the time you get to the center, there should be hardly any paint left on your brush, producing a very soft paint effect in this area.

STIPPLING TO SHADE WITH TWO COLORS

Using a reasonable amount of paint, apply the lighter shade first. Apply the darker shade to one side only of each window. (Here, the second color is applied to the right-hand side). A few dabs of the darker color paint is quite sufficient.

BASIC TECHNIQUES

FLICKING UPWARD WITH BRUSH

Using a reasonable amount of paint (not too wet or too dry) on your brush, flick upward only. This creates a line at the top of the petals and leaves.

FLICKING IN TWO DIRECTIONS

Using a reasonable amount of paint on your brush, flick up and down. Do not use too much paint, as it will collect on the edges.

FLICKING FROM THE OUTSIDE TO THE CENTER

Using a reasonable amount of paint on your brush, flick from the outside edges in to the center of the design. Flick from the top to the center, from the bottom to the center, from the left to the center, and from the right to the center.

FLICKING FROM THE TOP TO THE CENTER

Using a reasonable amount of paint, flick from the top edge of the window to the center of the design, then from the bottom edge to the center.

RIGHT-HAND DROP SHADOW

Apply the first color, which should be your lighter shade, using a block effect. Concentrate on one side of each window (here, the right-hand side). Move the stencil slightly to the left—a fraction of an inch is sufficient—taking care not to move it up or down. Block again, using a darker color.

STENCILING

TEMPLATES

Enlarge the templates on a photocopier, or trace the design and draw a grid of evenly spaced squares over your tracing. Draw a larger grid on another piece of paper and copy the outline square by square. Draw over the lines to make sure they are continuous.

Frosted Vases, pp. 8-10. Scale up.

STENCILING

Art Nouveau Hatbox, pp. 14-16. Scale up.

Star Frame, pp. 17-19. Same size.

Making Sandcastles, pp. 20-23. Scale up.

88

TEMPLATES

Seashore Bathroom Set, pp. 24-26. Same size.

Greek Urns, pp. 27-29. Same size.

89

STENCILING

French Country Kitchen, pp. 34-37. Same size.

Tray of Autumn Leaves, pp. 38-40. Same size.

Pennsylvania Dutch Tulips, pp. 30-33. Same size.

TEMPLATES

*Gilded Candles, pp. 41-43.
Same size.*

*Heraldic Dining
Room, pp. 66-69.
Scale up.*

*Renaissance
Art, pp. 44-47.
Scale up.*

91

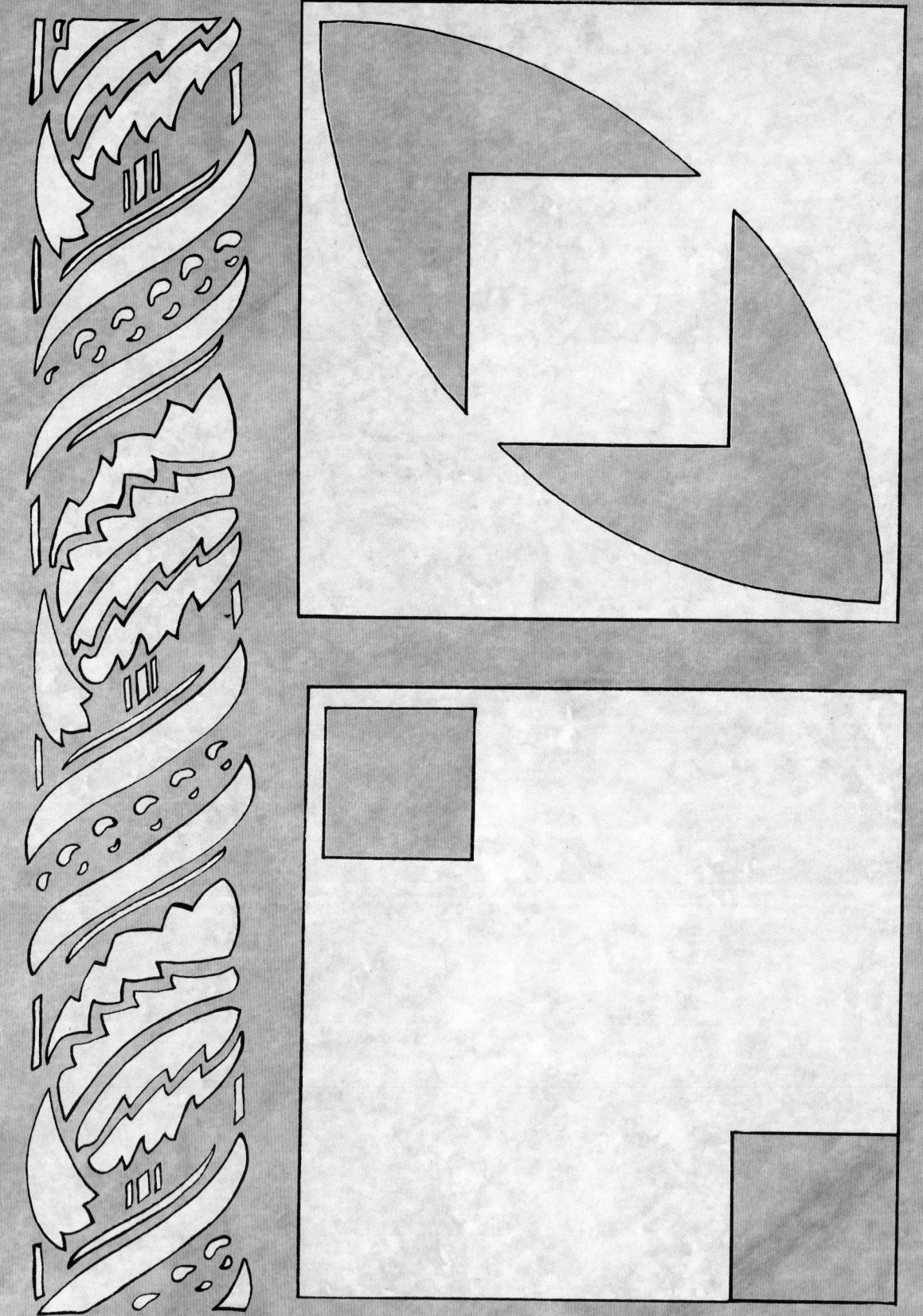

Geometric Floor Tiles, pp. 48-51. Scale up.

Organza Cushion, pp. 52-54. Scale up.

TEMPLATES

Through the Grapevine, pp. 58-61. Scale up.

Tablecloth and Napkins, pp. 55-57. Scale up.

93

TEMPLATES

Celestial Cherubs,
pp. 74-77.
Scale up.

*Rope and
Shells,*
pp. 62-65.
Scale up.

Trompe L'œil Plates,
pp. 70-73. *Scale up.*

SUPPLIERS

The specialty materials and equipment that you will require for the stenciling projects featured in this book are available at any good art-supply shop.

Adventures in Crafts
Yorkville Station
P. O. Box 6058
New York, NY 10128
(212) 410-9793

Art Essentials of New York Ltd
3 Cross Street
Suffern, NY 10901
(800) 283-5323

Createx Colors
14 Airport Park Road
East Granby, CT 06026
(860) 653-5505

Dick Blick
P.O. Box 1267
Galesburg, IL 61402
(309) 343-6181

Heartland Craft Discounters
Route 6 E., P. O. Box 65
Genesco, IL 61254
(309) 944-6411

Hofcraft
P. O. Box 72
Grand Haven, MI 49417
(800) 828-0359

Sandeen's
1315 White Bear Ave.
St. Paul, MN 55106
(612) 776-7012

Stencil House of New Hampshire
P. O. Box 16109
Hooksett, NH 03106
(603) 625-1716

ACKNOWLEDGMENTS

The publishers would like to thank the following people: Sacha Cohen for the Greek Urns, pp. 27-29, Through the Grapevine, pp. 58-61, Rope and Shells, pp. 62-65, Heraldic Dining Room, pp. 66-69; Petra Boase for the Frosted Vases, pp. 8-10, Painted Drawers, pp. 11-13, Star Frame, pp. 17-19, Making Sandcastles, pp. 20-23, Seashore Bathroom Set, pp. 24-26, Tablecloth and Napkins, pp. 55-57; Lucinda Ganderton for the Art Nouveau Hatbox, pp. 14-16, Pennsylvania Dutch Tulips, pp. 30-33, French Country Kitchen, pp. 34-37, Renaissance Art, pp. 44-47, Geometric Floor Tiles, pp. 48-51, Celestial Cherubs, pp. 74-77; Emma Hardy for the Tray of Autumn Leaves, pp. 38-40, Gilded Candles, pp. 41-43, Organza Cushion, pp. 52-54, Trompe L'œil Plates, pp. 70-73.

INDEX

acrylic stencil paint, 78
acrylic varnish, 78
Art Nouveau hatbox, 14-16
autumn leaves, tray of, 38-40

bathroom set, seashore, 24-26
block stenciling, 83
brushes, 80

candles, gilded, 41-43
cardboard, 80
cherubs, celestial, 74-77
containers, paint-mixing, 80
craft knives, 80
creams: metallic, 78
  oil-based, 78
curtains, French country kitchen, 34-37
cushion, organza, 52-54
cutting mats, 80
cutting stencils, 82

dining room, heraldic, 66-69
drawers, painted, 11-13
dry-brushing, 84, 85

equipment, 80-81
etching cream, frosted vases, 8-10

fabric paints, 78
flicking, 86
floor tiles, geometric, 48-51
frame, star, 17-19
French country kitchen, 34-37
frosted vases, 8-10

geometric floor tiles, 48-51
gilded candles, 41-43
glass, frosted vases, 8-10
gold, metallic creams, 78
gold leaf, 78
gold size, 78
grapevine, 58-61
Greek urns, 27-29

hatbox, Art Nouveau, 14-16
heraldic dining room, 66-69

latex paint, 78
leaves, tray of autumn, 38-40

masking tape, 80
materials, 78-79
metallic creams, 78

napkins, 55-57

oil-based stencil sticks and creams, 78
organza cushion, 52-54

paint-mixing container, 80
paints: acrylic stencil, 78
  fabric, 78
  latex, 78
pencils, 80
Pennsylvania Dutch tulips, 30-33
picture frame, star, 17-19
plates, trompe-l'œil, 70-73

Renaissance art, 44-47
rope and shells, 62-65
rotating stencils, 83-84

sandcastles, making, 20-23
seashore bathroom set, 24-26
shading, 83
shells and rope, 62-65
size, gold, 78
star frame, 17-19
stencil cardboard, 80
stippling, 85
straightedges, 80

tablecloth and napkins, 55-57
tape measures, 80
techniques, 82-86
templates, 87-94
  transferring, 82
through the grapevine, 58-61
tracing paper, 80
tray of autumn leaves, 38-40
trompe-l'œil plates, 70-73
tulips, Pennsylvania Dutch, 30-33

urns, Greek, 27-29

varnish, acrylic, 78
vases, frosted, 8-10